Walking With Saint James

31 Meditations for Pilgrims on the Camino de Santiago

ZEBULUN MATTOS

WALKING WITH SAINT JAMES

31 Meditations for Pilgrims on the Camino de Santiago

Zebulun Mattos

Nomad Creative Co.

Copyright © 2023 Zebulun Mattos

The information in this book was correct at the time of publication, but the Author does not assume any liability for loss or damage caused by errors or omissions. The personal anecdotes are the memories from his perspective, and he has tried to represent events as faithfully as possible.

Copyright © 2023 Zebulun Mattos All rights reserved.

No part of this book may be reproduced or used in any manner without the prior written permission of the copyright owner, except for the use of brief quotations.

To request permissions, you can contact the author at ZebulunMattos.com

First edition May 2023.

Early edits by Bernice Mattos and Megan Kappe
Final edits by Nomad Creative Co.
Art & Layout by Nomad Creative Co.

www.ZebulunMattos.com

All Bible text derived from the Literal Text found at unfoldingWord.org. It is licensed under a Creative Commons Attribution-Share Alike 4.0 International License. Original work available at unfoldingWord.org.

ENDORSEMENTS

"Reading Zebulun's book transports me back to that special place, taking me on a journey that my soul longs for."

- **Seth Barnes**, Founder and President of Adventures.org

"This exceptional book is an easy read. Zebulun has an uncanny ability to weave in the cultural aspects of the journey along with the more important spiritual aspects of Saint James' walk with the Lord, as well as our own journey with Christ. If you plan on doing a pilgrimage on the Camino de Santiago with the intent of growing closer to Christ, then this book will absolutely be of great benefit to you!"

- **Gary Stache**, Pastor

"This book, like its author, is adventurous, unorthodox, and invites the reader on a journey into a deeper spiritual life. A brilliant read!"

- **Darren Davis**, Senior Leader at Harbour South Florida

"A stunning work with simplicity and clarity! Zebulun's storytelling makes you feel like you're walking the Camino de Santiago on a sacred journey yourself. Uplifting and compelling, I absolutely loved reading this book!"

- **Noulezhalie Ricky Medom**

"Zebulun takes us on a journey of passion, faith, courage, and perseverance to discover that the Camino de Santiago points us to a place of peace and solitude through God's amazing presence."

- **Mel Santiago**, Musician

"When the modern pilgrimage has been replaced by the long road trip, it's good to be reminded of the real and ancient pilgrimages that are still out there to be experienced. Zebulun invites us to walk with him and Jesus on his journey. Great book…reminded me of my own God given pilgrimage many years ago across Europe, Africa, and the Middle East. Same trials, pains, challenges, and blessings of the pilgrim."

- **Grady Pickett**, Pastor and CEO of Faith Frontiers

"It has been, and still is, a dream of mine to walk the Camino. *Walking with Saint James* is a breath of fresh air as I consider one day walking it myself. When I do, Zebulun will be my companion through this book. This book should be required reading for everyone who is interested in walking the Camino de Santiago, past, present, or future!"

- **Gary Thomas**, Spiritual Director

To you: my fellow pilgrim.

Ultreïa!

Keep moving forward...

"At times you will walk by yourself; but you will never walk alone."

- PILGRIM SAYING ON THE CAMINO DE SANTIAGO

FOREWORD

Of all the places on the Camino that I hiked with Zebulun ten years ago, the path we walked out of *O Cebreiro* stands out to me. As usual, we left in darkness. The cold penetrated down to our bones until we got a pace going and found ourselves singing as we hiked.

"The sun comes up, it's a new day dawning;
It's time to sing Your song again.
Whatever may pass and whatever lies before me,
Let me be singing when the evening comes."

Soon, the rhythms of the Camino had enfolded us afresh. And as the new day began to dawn, it revealed the spectacle of verdant valleys enshrouded in mist that beckoned us deeper into a world we couldn't see but seemed to welcome us at every bend.

We need journeys like that to reinvigorate our spirits, and we need guides like Zebulun Mattos to accompany us and help us to fathom all that God would reveal to us along our path.

In "Walking with Saint James," Zebulun draws on our experience along the *Camino de Santiago* a decade past for inspiration. The guidance he offers comes from his own steps along the way as well as from Scripture. It's possible to hike the entire 500 miles in a month, and Zebulun offers meditations for each day.

So much about the *Camino* is special. The daily rhythms simplify your life. When it's time to stop for a midmorning *café con leche* with a chocolate croissant, the world somehow looks as it should as you assimilate Camino culture.

I remember at our first stop, there were a number of *peregrinos* sitting outside in the morning sun. We were warmly greeted by a group we'd already gotten to know.

There was Edward, the Russian who had been kicked out of the house by his wife who was tired of his wine drinking. He had a bottle of wine sitting on the table beside a cappuccino.

There was the couple who had only met on the Camino five days earlier but now were in love.

Later we would meet Sylvia, the 31-year-old mother of three from Germany hiking with 19-year-old Albert from Venice, and Fabio, a Franciscan friar who became an honorary member of our group and Mike, the venture capitalist.

Everyone is on an equal footing while walking the Camino. Each has their own reasons for going. Each sleeps in the same common rooms along the way, and each lives the simple life that the Camino requires of those who walk it.

Evening times can be a delight if someone has a guitar along, and those gathered are able to sing.

The days inevitably hold surprises as you find yourself passing through quaint towns or passing locals who cheer you on with cries of "Buen Camino!"

Hiking the Camino is a life within a life. You live episodes every day. The history of this pilgrimage may go back more than a millennium, but its culture is still evolving every day. And as we hike it, all who are *peregrinos* are also co-creators.

Returning from the Camino, I found that I'd fallen in love again with simplicity, community, and grace. I returned to people I love living a lifestyle in America that had grown too rushed and complicated. When I returned, I found myself walking more, walking into a lifestyle that reminded me of this road I left.

In the meantime, reading Zebulun's book transports me back to that special place, taking me on a journey that my soul longs for. I need the grace of its rhythms and people. Maybe one day you can join Zebulun on the Camino, and if not in Spain, then maybe on the road to greater grace.

Seth Barnes
Founder and President of Adventures.org

INTRODUCTION

Always take the alternate path.

- Pilgrim saying on the Camino de Santiago

The Camino de Santiago, or the Way of Saint James, is a pilgrimage that concludes in the northwestern Spanish city of Santiago de Compostela at the tomb of Saint James. For more than twelve hundred years, the shrine of Saint James has been visited by millions of pilgrims, making it one of the oldest and most popular Christian pilgrimage sites in the world.

The current burial place of the relics of Saint James is located in a vault under a Catholic cathedral called the *Santiago de Compostela Cathedral*. The present-day basilica took over 130 years to build and was consecrated in the year 1211 at the height of the Middle Ages.

The Camino de Santiago has been traversed by countless pilgrims who embark on this journey for a plethora of reasons. Each pilgrim sets out on a sacred quest in search of meaning, healing, restoration, or sometimes just for the sheer thrill of the challenge. Pilgrims can choose their own route and will, ultimately, walk in the footsteps of those who have gone before them.

The actual walkway of the Camino itself is comprised of a matrix of footpaths that weave through scenic towns and charming villages throughout the Spanish or Portuguese countryside.

One major route is the *Vía de la Plata* route, which starts in the south of Spain. Another route is the coastal Portuguese

Camino, where the pilgrim walks through Portugal and finishes in Spain. There is also the Camino del Norte that follows along the northern coast of Spain in a parallel fashion before turning downward towards Santiago de Compostela.

The most popular route taken by pilgrims is the 500-mile (800-kilometer) *Camino Francés,* or the French Way. It begins just north of the Spanish border in the foothills of the French side of the Pyrenees Mountains.

Pilgrims taking this route will begin their hike out of the old town of Saint-Jean-Pied-de-Port and make their way southward, trekking over the Pyrenees. At the end of their first day, they will stay in or near the Spanish town of Roncesvalles before continuing on through four regions of Spain. Listed in geographic order, these four autonomous regions were once the independent kingdoms of Navarre, La Rioja, Castile & León, and finally Galicia, home to the stunning Cathedral of Saint James. Depending on many factors, the entire journey by foot will take somewhere between 30 and 40 days, sometimes more.

Who Wrote the Epistle of James?

Before we continue, it is important to acknowledge that the actual author of the Book of James, found in the New Testament, remains uncertain. This uncertainty primarily stems from the popularity of the name James, which was shared by two of the 12 apostles of Christ. Although we know with certainty that the short book was indeed written by a James, scholars remain unsure if the author was James the Just (brother of Christ) or James the Great (brother of John). The debate persists to this day.

Until definitive evidence is produced and examined, we must rest in the tensions of this mystery, recognizing that there is much to learn from the writings of Saint James, who was a student of Christ Himself.

For now, let's briefly examine both men to satisfy our curiosities.

The first James we will consider is James, the brother of Jesus (although some traditions assert that he was merely Jesus's cousin, not his actual blood brother). He was also known as James the Just or James the Less and was renowned for his wisdom and virtue. It is believed that James, the brother of Jesus, was stoned to death in Jerusalem.

The other James in question had a brother named John. Both men were among the original 12 disciples of Christ. This James is known as James the Great and, later, became the patron saint of Spain. The two brothers, sons of a fisherman named Zebedee, were known for their quick tempers and zealous demeanors. In fact, they were nicknamed the Sons of Thunder due to these traits. James and his brother were among the first called by Jesus to travel with Him and be His disciples, a teaching method customary at the time for instructors of philosophy and religion.

In one humorous anecdote, James and John brought their mother to Jesus. She requested on their behalf that once Jesus had conquered the kingdoms of the world and established Himself as King of the Earth, her sons be the ones to sit next to Him on the King's throne as His two right-hand men. Jesus, patient with them and aware that they did not yet grasp the full picture, replied, "You don't know what you're asking."

On another occasion, as the group of disciples journeyed toward Jerusalem, the holy city, they stopped in a Samaritan village. Since Samaritans were half-Gentile, it was taboo for the disciples to be there according . They attempted to explain that Jesus was the promised Messiah, but the townspeople refused to welcome Him. The brothers then suggested that Jesus call down fire from heaven and burn up the village. Once again, Jesus had to temper their passionate outbursts.

While we cannot determine the actual author with certainty, we can still discern his passionate personality throughout the writings. For James, everything is black and white; there is no gray area or middle ground. Although his austere tone may seem foreign to some modern readers, the author urges readers to maintain an open mind, as wisdom lies within his writings.

After Jesus Christ was crucified and resurrected, tradition holds that James, the brother of John, journeyed to the Iberian Peninsula to spread Christ's redemptive message. After some time in *Hispania*, the farthest western reach of the Roman Empire, he returned to Jerusalem. He was subsequently captured and martyred by King Herod Agrippa I of Judea.

His body was brought back to Spain, and through a series of events, was ultimately laid to rest in the crypt beneath what is now the Santiago de Compostela Cathedral. It is to this sacred site that weary pilgrims from around the world complete their long and arduous journey.

Though the author's assumption is that James the Great and the author of the Epistle of James are one and the same, this may not ultimately be the case. Only time will reveal the truth.

While the debate over the true authorship of the Book of James may persist, his influence remains indisputable. The writings of Saint James provide timeless perspectives on leading a virtuous life. His writings also offer both challenges and encouragement to believers to persevere in their quest for a deeper relationship with Christ. By studying and reflecting upon these teachings, we can continue to progress in our own spiritual journey, drawing closer to the ultimate source of truth and salvation: Jesus Christ.

Symbols on the Camino
There are several traditions that symbolize milestones along *the Way*. Every pilgrim is to bring a small pebble from their home country. They will leave this stone, symbolic of their burdens, at the foot of a designated landmark cross many days into their journey.

In another tradition, pilgrims acquire a scallop shell, which is a symbol of a pilgrim who is currently embarking on, or has already undertaken this great pilgrimage.

Finally, the modern pilgrim is given a little Camino passport, or *credencial.* It is reminiscent of the letter of safe passage once granted to pilgrims of old. At each pilgrim hostel, or *albergue*, where they rest for the night, a stamp unique to that place is pressed into this passport. After the pilgrim has finished the Camino, they will take this collection of stamps to the registrar's office where they then receive their *compostela*, the pilgrim's certificate of completion.

Saints and pilgrims alike look to Christ for guidance along *the Way*. Christ is our ultimate example and did a masterful job at not only speaking few words, but also coupled them with actions done in love. Saint James learned from this and wrote about it in his letter.

As we begin our journey on the Camino de Santiago, may our hearts be attentive to God's voice within. May we be filled with His presence and peace. May we shine the light of His Truth and Gospel in love to those we encounter on the Camino and beyond.

These following meditations were written for you, dear pilgrim, wherever you are on life's journey. Maybe one day you will embark on the Camino yourself, or perhaps you have already walked its ancient paths. No matter where your own journey takes you, remember you are loved by God and by your fellow pilgrims.

And as we walk this path together, let us love God and one another. May our hearts seek the One from which our spirits were born.

¡Buen Camino!

Christ with me,
Christ before me,
Christ behind me,
Christ within me,
Christ beneath me,
Christ above me,
Christ on my right,
Christ on my left,
Christ when I lie down,
Christ when I sit down.

- Prayer by Saint Patrick of Ireland

HOW TO READ THIS BOOK

This book is not meant to serve as a tourist guide for the Camino, but as a companion for pilgrims on their spiritual journey.

It is designed to be read one day at a time, like a daily devotional. Each day consists of anecdotes from the author's own Camino experience, followed by a *Camino Contemplation* that weaves in thoughts from the writings of Saint James.

The author then offers a one or two sentence *Practical Application* summarizing the day's spiritual insights, followed by a direct quote from Saint James, and, finally, a *Prayer for the Peregrino*. This order is repeated the following day.

The author intentionally refers to himself in the third person as the Pilgrim, with a capital "P," to minimize distractions. While the audio version does not make this distinction, it can be inferred from the context.

WHY THIS BOOK

The author's journey on the Camino de Santiago began not in France, where he had wanted to start, but in Belorado, nearly 140 miles beyond the traditional starting point.

Unbeknownst to him at the time, this journey would prove both challenging and life-changing. It served as a sacred space for healing, growth, and spiritual discipline.

Over the weeks, the Pilgrim read through the letter written by the beloved saint. He realized that, despite walking the Way of Saint James, there wasn't much information about Saint James himself along the way, other than some extravagant tales of James returning as a would-be crusader. Of course, James would be honored and venerated with the utmost esteem at the Cathedral of Santiago de Compostela, but little was said about him or his writings along the way. Although the Pilgrim didn't know at the time that the authorship of the Biblical book of James was contested, he recognized the value in learning from James' writings.

Eager to truly grasp the essence of what James had written, the Pilgrim asked God for wisdom and clarity to understand. As he read, he jotted down thoughts and observations. This book is the culmination of that quiet time of reflection.

Finding Redemption
Although the Book of James is quite short, with only five chapters, Saint James reveals his passionate heart. He had experienced life before Christ and learned that life with Christ was better. He urges readers to abandon trust in their own

wisdom and instead seek a better reality, as he had discovered while walking with Jesus.

Long-time followers of the Way of Christ can attest that this liberating truth is indeed a better path, leading to a life of peace, joy, and ultimate fulfillment. Redemption is not attained through our own good deeds, but by trusting that the death-debt we owe due to our transgressions was paid for by Jesus when He died on the Cross, and that it is sufficient. Jesus Christ's resurrection, three days after being buried in the tomb in Jerusalem, has brought hope and life—real life—to countless people worldwide. In fact, it can be argued that Jesus' message is the only message of true and selfless love in the world, where the self is not the subject and reason for life, but God is. Our ego is laid to waste in the face of this reality.

God, incarnate as Jesus Christ, bestowed this gift, proclaiming that you are blessed and highly favored by God, regardless of who you are or what you've done. A gift is simply received, never earned. We are challenged to trust Jesus in this message, just as James did. Trusting in Jesus prompts a transformation within our hearts, likened to being born anew with a clean slate and a fresh start. Saint James believed this message and strives to persuade us to become believers so that we too might find redemption.

Since Saint James wrote a letter for us, the author believes that we will honor him and others who have embarked on this pilgrimage by reading and learning from what he wrote.

TERMS & TRANSLATIONS

While interchangeable, this publication uses a mix of terms in Spanish and English at different times. The purpose is to draw an authentic feel to life in Spain along the *Camino* for the Pilgrim's journey.

Peregrino - Pilgrim

Albergue - Hostel for pilgrims

Camino - Way, path, journey

Camino De Santiago - Way of Saint James

Santiago - James / Saint James

¡Buen Camino! - Greeting: "Have a good Journey"

The Pilgrim - with a capitalized "P", referring to the author of this book; lowercase "p" refers to pilgrims in general

Santiago de Compostela - A city in northwestern Spain; also the Cathedral of Saint James

Finisterre - "The end of the world", the name of the cape a few days walk past Santiago de Compostela

Refugio - a refuge, another term for a pilgrim hostel

Romanesque - a term referring to the simple and symmetrical architectural design of Medieval Europe, beginning around the tenth century AD and lasting until the thirteenth century. It is characterized by towering semi-circular arches, small windows, massive barrel vaulting, thick and solid walls, and enormous sturdy pillars.

Gothic - a term referring to the architectural design that developed from Romanesque. It is similar to the Romanesque style but is more stylized in design and was mostly used from the twelfth to the sixteenth centuries. It is characterized by the definitive pointed arch. The Burgos Cathedral is an example of Gothic architecture.

Baroque - Arising out of the Counter-Reformation in the sixteenth century and lasting until the eighteenth century, Baroque architecture combined the robust quality of Romanesque, the intricate designs of Gothic, and introduced a strong element of bewildering artistic embellishment and decoration into the design as a kind of visual storytelling technique, which helped illiterate people better understand Biblical stories.

Mudéjar Design - A richly ornate decoration style characterized by intricate geometric motifs, elegant vegetal shapes, and stylized pseudo-Kufic calligraphy that resembles Arab lettering but doesn't actually have any meaning. This style emerged as a fusion of Islamic and Christian artistic elements during the time when Muslims and Christians coexisted in the Iberian Peninsula.

Hostelier - A person who owns or runs a hostel.

Mozárab (or Mozarabic) - A term referring to the Christians living in the Iberian Peninsula under Moorish (Islamic) rule during the medieval period, the distinctive form of art and architecture created by these Christians that often incorporated elements of Islamic design, as well as the language spoken by these Christians, which was a Romance dialect influenced by Arabic vocabulary and grammar.

Codex Calixtinus - a medieval manuscript, also known as the *Liber Sancti Jacobi*, that was created in the 12th century as a liturgical and historical guide for pilgrims on the Camino de

Santiago. It contains a wealth of information on the pilgrimage, including descriptions of the route, advice for pilgrims, and liturgical texts. The Codex is also notable for containing the first known collection of polyphonic music. It is named after Pope Callixtus II, who was pope at the time the manuscript was created.

ZEBULUN MATTOS

FIRST DAY

"There is no moment of delight in any
pilgrimage like the beginning of it."

- Charles Dudley, Eighteenth-century American politician

The Beginning...

Pilgrims who have started in France will cross a bridge over the Nive River and face a steep climb further up into the beautiful, but sometimes cold, mountains. They will walk through a mountain pass where, in the year 778, Charlemagne's army was attacked and defeated. The victorious Basques still reside in the region. Then, each pilgrim will walk a few hours before seeking shelter and resting that first night on the border in Orisson, France, or crossing into Spain and finding a *refugio* in Roncesvalles, Spain.

Moving through the hills that flow out of the Pyrenees and into the Iberian Peninsula, individual pilgrims walking step by step along the ancient path ultimately share one simple desire: to finish! This aspiration, shared by all pilgrims since the beginning, brings with it a breathless and deeply personal prayer: *Lord, grant me the strength to complete this journey.* Their path chosen is special. Some might suggest that it was the Path that chose the pilgrim! Whatever their reason, they are here, and their quest has begun.

The anthropological history of this region of the world is ancient. At times, it can feel like one has stepped back in time a thousand years. Although the digital world of modern technology threatens to obscure the analog world of old, the ageless beauty of the distant past has somehow held on through dutiful resolve. Those who dream of the simple ways of yesterday preserve this explicit beauty within their culture. Ancient wisdom sustains and protects the youthful vigor of today's modern Camino. It is on the Camino de Santiago that we find that the old and the new are weaving a magnificent story.

The world of the pilgrim's path is filled with wonderful architecture and monuments and captivating stories and tales. The compelling culinary delights each offer a unique flavor that has been passed down from generation to generation into the hands that received it, and now we get to enjoy it today.

In the collective fibers and tidbits of this grand story, we find that the threads of the pilgrim are being crafted, stitch by stitch, as individual threads into a collective tapestry of meaning. Old paths blend with new ones.

Each pilgrim bears a revealing sign of pilgrimage with their backpack, walking sticks, and scallop shell marked with the red Cross of Saint James. A casual outside observer might think us all the same, but we are not. Our stories are unique, but we share a common bond of travail, the threads of adventure, and a search for deeper meaning. In walking the Camino de Santiago, we find significance in life. The pilgrim soul is invigorated and sustained by this journey. It will be a memory that revives the pilgrim spirit and will sustain them for the rest of their lives.

Whether the journey begins in the foothills at Roncesvalles or a bit farther down the road by way of Jaca in neighboring Aragón province, each will undoubtedly walk through Puente la Reina, a town south of Pamplona, which is the city famed throughout the world for its annual run with the bulls each July.

The Camino, running parallel to the Spanish northern shoreline along the swelling Bay of Biscay, continues in a westerly direction towards the shores of Cape Finisterre. Beyond that lies the mighty Atlantic Ocean. Descending from the southern face of the snowcapped Pyrenees, the land slopes downward, forming the Ebro Basin. This is the heart of the old Basque Country, a land with a unique culture of its own. The unpretentious ways of the Basque farmers involve regularly cooking together in groups, sipping homemade cider from the bountiful apple trees that thrive in Spain, and savoring freshly caught Atlantic cod and pungent sheep's milk cheeses.

The pilgrimage offers an opportunity for sojourners to traverse beneath splendid arches, across ancient bridges, and alongside numerous crosses that beckon each pilgrim to reach heavenward and inward along the way. Enigmatic monuments, ruins, castles, and churches stand as testaments to a mysterious past, each with a story just waiting to be uncovered. The footpath meanders over countless rivers and streams, through endless fields of grain, bountiful farmland, and sandy valleys abundant with vineyards and beasts of burden laboring under the hot Spanish sun.

At times, the pilgrim's hardships are eased by a fleeting break from the sun's intensity, as they stroll beneath the cool shade of oak, beech, and willow trees. The province of Navarra's landscape is adorned with blackberry patches that flourish in the low hills, as well as across the pine-covered highlands of various massifs within the densely clustered Basque Mountain range. The region's streams and rivers essentially serve as tributaries to the Ebro River, Spain's longest river flowing entirely within its borders. The Ebro River embarks on its own journey among the Spanish Cantabrian Mountains, nourished by the entirety of the southern Pyrenees up to the Spanish region of Andorra. It then continues its flow southeast towards North Africa, eventually emptying into the Mediterranean Sea at its delta in the autonomous region of Catalonia.

Camino Contemplation

Saint James emphasized in his writings that hardships are inevitable, and that we should embrace these challenges as catalysts to help us thrive in life. The Camino de Santiago, it must be said, is not an easy journey. By embarking on this pilgrimage, we put our entire being to the test; our mind, spirit, soul, and body.

The Camino de Santiago is lengthy and, at times, perilous. We must tread carefully and attentively, always looking ahead, while directing our spiritual gaze inward to listen and heed the still small voice that is guiding us along the way.

Saint James was well-acquainted with this spiritual path and sought Christ for guidance and solace. The roads along the Camino are rugged and winding, encompassing mountains, valleys, forests, and deserts that each pilgrim must navigate. The paths are sometimes just wide enough for two people to walk side by side, reminiscent of the *straight and narrow*. Danger, hardships, and trials may present themselves, but we keep our eyes focused straight ahead. With single-minded determination, we concentrate on one goal: *reaching the end*, which symbolizes reuniting and becoming unified with Jesus.

Practical Application

Life will be hard, even if you follow Jesus. But only Christ can give you the inner strength needed to endure each challenge. So lean on Christ and his strength every day.

St. James writes:

James 1:1 *I, James, serve God and am bound to God through the Lord Jesus Christ. I am writing this letter to the twelve Jewish tribes who trust in Christ and who are scattered throughout the world. I greet you all.* ***2*** *My fellow believers, consider it something to greatly rejoice over when you experience various kinds of hardships.* ***3*** *Understand that as you trust God in hardships, they help you to endure even* *more hardships. **4** Endure hardships to their very end, so that you may follow Christ in every way. Then you will not fail to do well.*

Prayer for the Peregrino:

Dear Lord, as I walk this journey with You, I ask for Your grace to finish every day. May I be filled with the same vision You had to finish Your journey and may I be filled with Your gratitude along the way. Thank you for walking alongside me.

In Christ's Name, Amen.

SECOND DAY

"And what is this valley called?"

"We call it now simply Wisdom's Valley: but the oldest maps mark it as the Valley of Humiliation."

- C.S. Lewis, The Pilgrim's Regress

Entering the Autonomous Region of La Rioja

At the bottom of the Ebro River basin lies the city of Logroño, where pilgrims cross from the Navarra region into La Rioja, a region known for its production of ceramics and native Tempranillo grapes growing in private family vineyards. Before modern techniques, this red wine, with its spicy flavors of tobacco, fruity plum, and fig, was mainly stored in the many caves and cavernous hollows hidden throughout the region.

The landscape transforms into undulating hillsides and gullies covered with thickets of oak, pine, and black poplars. There are vast cultivated areas growing cash crops like sunflowers, rye, barley, and, of course, grapevines. The avian population becomes more diverse, with possible sightings of short-tailed partridges, bright yellow goldfinches, and melodious larks darting amongst the bushes and singing while flittering through the sky.

Along the eroded hillsides grow aromatic thyme, long esparto grass used in basket weaving since ancient times, and star-shaped aster, which likes to bloom purple in the autumn. The path now runs beneath the coastal Cantabrian Mountain range, still parallel to the stormy waters of the North Atlantic Ocean.

Built along the Tirón River, a tributary to the Ebro River, where the Ayago Mountains turn into foothills, Belorado is an old stone village topped with red roofs and studded with TV antennae.

Entering the village in the second week of May, the Pilgrim explored the ninth-century ruins of the Castle of Belorado. Having not yet exhausted the strength in his legs to climb the hill on which it sat, he stood amongst the rubble in the old hill fort that had fallen into terrible disrepair.

Sweeping views of both the rural village below and the surrounding countryside tied together a feeling of antiquity and the present modern life. It was a significant perch, providing both an overview of the village below and a panorama of the sprawling countryside.

A deserted field, recently harvested and overgrown with grass, led from the old fortress. Wind turbines stood erect, nearly motionless in the backdrop. Lying supine in the tall esparto grass, he watched the clouds effortlessly meander on in great billows of mist and water vapor. The Pilgrim's mind wandered to the journey ahead. What would it look like? The stream of time slowed to a trickle, almost palpable. Pulling his fingers through the flow, he closed his eyes for a moment in solitary bliss.

The decaying monument, long since abandoned, spoke a silent story of cruel battles fought, and it whispered an inaudible recounting of bygone years. Once upon a time, life had been abundant in this place. Now, it appeared empty. But was it really devoid of life?

Looking at the field and plants growing in the cracks of the crumbling fortress, the pilgrim realized that life indeed was still abundant here; it just looked different from before.

But that bliss wouldn't last forever.

Rising from that peaceful grassland overlooking Belorado, he searched for the path that led downward and off the hill. Several mates would meet up with him very soon. Together, they would walk the remaining 300 miles of the Camino.

Taking one last gaze at the ruins of the old castle on the way down, he paused to take it in knowing it would likely be his last chance to see the world from this perspective in this place. Straining to hear more of the *murmur of antiquity*, he got distracted by the crumbling footpath beneath his feet and failed to recall this place again until some time had passed.

Camino Contemplation

Before becoming a saint, James had been a fisherman and was undoubtedly familiar with the often turbulent Sea of Galilee, as well as the vast Mediterranean Sea.

Growing up near the coast, James understood the temperamental nature of the water and would have appreciated the immense beauty and constant motion of waves rippling towards the shore.

Spending time out at sea and away from the coast, James observed that waves showed no perceptible direction of flow. Waves were tossed to and fro, going this way and that, influenced by the wind and, as we now know scientifically, the gravitational pull of the moon.

The journey on the Camino de Santiago is challenging and life-changing. It is sacred—a space of healing, growth, and spiritual discipline. Saint James knew that God is good and generous. He warns us to be aware of the winds of distraction that might sidetrack us and turn us away from our own sacred journey. He teaches us to directly ask God for wisdom, and God will help us figure out what to do next!

Two sound pieces of advice from Saint James support us in our daily lives: ask and believe. If you need help making a decision in life, ask God for wisdom. And when you ask, trust that God will genuinely guide you!

Then he adds a bonus third: If you say you follow Christ, then don't be apathetic. Instead, be fully committed, seeking wisdom from above, which is given freely and without prejudice. Expect to hear from heaven, and don't doubt. For doubt is like a directionless wave in the middle of the sea.

Practical Application

God is generous. When you need wisdom for the journey, just ask him and trust him to make good on his word.

St. James Writes

James 1: 5 If any one of you needs to know what to do, let him ask God, who gives generously and is not angry at anyone who asks. 6 But when you ask God, trust him to answer you. Do not doubt that he will answer and always help you, because people who keep doubting

*God cannot follow him, like a wave of the sea that is blown back and forth by the wind and thus cannot continue in the same direction. **7** Indeed, people who doubt should not think that the Lord God will do anything that they request him to do. **8** For they are people who cannot decide whether they will follow Jesus or not follow Jesus. These people do not do what they say they will do.*

Prayer for the Peregrino

Lord, I seek Your freely-given wisdom in all moments of my daily life. As I walk this path today, please give me wisdom to love, and forgive, both myself and others. Help me to stay true to Your path in the way You have shown me.

In Christ's Name, Amen.

THIRD DAY

> "One of the dangers of having a lot of money is that you may be quite satisfied with the kinds of happiness money can give and so fail to realize your need for God. If everything seems to come simply by signing checks, you may forget that you are at every moment totally dependent on God."
>
> - C.S. Lewis, Mere Christianity

The Path from Belorado to San Juan de Ortega

At sunrise the next morning, the Pilgrim joined the others in preparing for the day's journey. The day started off cold and rainy, with the ground covered in a thin layer of hail. Like any other day, the experienced pilgrims prepared for the day's walk in their own ways. Already a week or so into their journeys, these pilgrims had settled into the cadence of the journey.

Outside, it continued drizzling. Inside, a chilly mist sent each pilgrim on a hunt to find a cup of hot coffee or tea. In spite of the fact that it was sprinkling and cold outside, the Pilgrim was eager to get going and stopped to chat with another pilgrim named Marcela. She was a tall, middle-aged Spaniard with dark hair draped in a ponytail from beneath her hat. Wrinkles in the corners of her eyes hinted at years of laughter.

"Buenos Dias!" She exclaimed. "Is this your first time on the Camino?"

"Today is the first day of my first time on the Camino," the Pilgrim informed her.

Her smiling eyes widened at this. This was an unusual starting place for a peregrino. Tucking her walking sticks beneath her arm, she reached into her backpack and pulled out several small clear pouches of nuts and seeds. She then handed them to the Pilgrim.

"Here," she said, placing them into the palm of his hand, "a gift for you!"

"Thank you!" He said.

Examining them closely, he identified raw walnuts, pecans, and another type of seed he had never seen before.

Inquiring as to what the mystery seeds were, she laughed and informed him that they were Spanish *piñones* or pine nuts. "Try them!" He grabbed a few pine nuts from the bag and tasted them. His eyes widened. They were tender, almost succulent. Their aroma was subtle, like pine. It filled the mouth with a delightful, buttery-citrus tang.

"These are delicious!" the Pilgrim exclaimed. Worried that she would not have enough, he added, "But won't you need these for your own journey?"

"No," Marcela replied. "You will need them more than I do. Today is my last day walking."

The Pilgrim wondered if something had happened to make her stop so far from the destination.

She explained that every year, during a vacation from work, she walks a portion of the Camino. "One day," she said with hopeful determination, "I hope to finish walking all 800 kilometers."

They exchanged hugs and wished each other a *Buen Camino*!

Inspired by her kindness, the Pilgrim knew this was a good beginning to a long journey. He felt grateful and was humbled by her generosity. Putting the food into his pocket, he grabbed his walking stick and took his first steps onto the ancient way of pilgrims. Listening to the sound his shoes made as they crunched the gravel underneath, the Pilgrim smiled.

And thus, the journey began.

As Marcela's journey came to a close, his journey was just beginning. Knowing the path would be rough at times, the Pilgrim ventured onward. He knew there would be steep mountain ranges to cross, thick forests to traverse, and desert wastelands to pass through. There would be rain, cold snow, and countless rivers to pass over. There would be little villages and big cities that he would anonymously walk through; just another pilgrim on the Way of St. James.

As the late morning sun burned away the mist, the wind turbines could be seen, most motionless in the windless backdrop of the rolling hillsides. Along the way, in the little village of Tosantos outside Belorado, a small cave church was built into the cliffside. Beyond this, the Camino transformed into a beautiful upward hike through the verdant forests of pine trees that protected each pilgrim along the way.

Camino Contemplation

Saint James spent three years under the direct tutelage of Christ. In his famous sermons about Being and Attitudes, Jesus taught that the poor in spirit are blessed by God because the Kingdom of Heaven belongs to them. Saint James helps us go a little deeper with this message.

On the one hand there is a *spirit of poverty* and on the other hand there is being *poor in spirit*. These two are similar in name but are fundamentally in opposition to one another. The first, *spirit of poverty*, has a selfish mindset and wrongly believes that there is never enough. It is a poor attitude to have that is prideful because it assumes that *self* is the rewarder of faith. The second one that Jesus taught, being *poor in spirit*, is a humble mindset rooted in Christ as the rewarder of faith and the giver of all good things. It is a mindset that trusts that God will provide for every need. It matters not if one's net worth is abundant, or meager. As another Biblical author put it, "God supplies all our needs according to the riches in glory in Christ Jesus."

One mindset is that of *pride*. The other, that of *humility, and trust*.

Saint James knew that money as a practical tool used every day is important. Money is neither good nor bad in and of itself. He helps give us a healthy framework so that money does not become what we worship.

Rich people die, and poor people die. Saint James teaches us that the amount of money we have does not matter. What matters is that we are honored by God when we are poor because we have to trust in Jesus Christ to provide, often a humiliating endeavor. What matters is that God humbles us when we are rich because we have to trust in Jesus Christ even more since all material wealth will one day wither and disappear.

Many pilgrims are not wealthy by the world's standards, but through simple faith and selfless acts of kindness and generosity along the way, many are made rich.

Practical Application

No matter your financial standing, poverty and riches mean nothing if you don't also trust Christ for help in your daily life.

St. James Writes

James 1: *9 Believers who are poor should be glad because God has honored them. 10 And believers who are rich should be glad that God has humbled them, which helps them trust in Jesus Christ, because they and their riches will pass away, just like wild flowers wither. 11 When the sun rises, the scorching hot wind dries the plants and causes the flowers to fall and no longer be beautiful. Like the flower that dies, rich people will die while they are earning money.*

Prayer for the Peregrino

Dear Lord Jesus, thank you for giving me a fresh perspective. Thank you for being trustworthy. I ask that You help me to keep my eyes on You, and not on the amount of wealth I have or don't have. May I be generous with what You have given to me. Life in You is the only true wealth.

In Christ's Name, Amen.

FOURTH DAY

"Jesus takes every believer on faith-building journeys where we learn to pray, receive, and trust."

- Mike Hudgins, Pastor

The Path from St. Juan de Ortega to Burgos

The cold stone floor of the monastery's guest room refused to warm in the dawn's early light. Smelling of musk and wet earth, the large room was lined with bunkbeds and served as the *albergue*, or the pilgrim's hostel. Throughout the night, reverberating snores of weary pilgrims remained locked within the rock walls. When the noisy sleepers turned to their sides and all grew quiet, owls took up the call of the night.

Sliding his shoes on, the groggy Pilgrim longed for a hot coffee and a warm breakfast. It was too early and the small adjacent restaurant had not yet opened. The Pilgrim was forced to continue on his way hungry. Only while passing through a little town called Ages was an eatery found. A handful of walnuts and *piñones* from Marcela sustained him until this point.

Leading out of the village, the land rose suddenly, and then began to slope gently downward providing a picturesque overlook of the city of *Burgos*. Walking on modern roads proved a significant challenge, more so than the gravel and dirt paths of old. Without the softness of the dirt paths, the body feels additional fatigue with each step. The Pilgrim suffered while walking the length of Burgos as the Camino path through the city consists of only concrete and pavement.

When compared to the countless countryside settlements of antiquity that pilgrims pass through, Burgos itself is a magnificently busy city and offers a wide variety of gastronomic delights. It is a point of convergence, where the old paths from the south meet together and continue as one towards *Santiago de Compostela*, and beyond that *Finisterre,* the very edge of the world.

The six floors of the modern La Casa Del Cubo albergue had good wifi, as well as modern showers and toilets. It was communal style with lots of bunkbeds and dozens of people in each large room. The albergue was situated next to the famed Gothic *Cathedral of Burgos* whose construction began in the early parts of the thirteenth century. It had replaced an original cathedral built almost two centuries earlier.

Exploring the city's narrow cobblestone streets and medieval pathways in the evening, the Pilgrim gazed with appreciation at the magnificent *Cathedral of St. Mary*. Famous for housing the tomb of El Cid, a military commander, and folk-hero who recaptured the region of Valencia from the Moors in the late eleventh century, the cathedral has three bell towers that are ornately designed in the spirit of French Gothic architecture, like many of the buildings in the area.

Flamboyant limestone spires, pinnacles, and arches designed with medieval flair speak of man's search for God while reaching towards the heavens. A splendid rose window predominates the main façade. Its circle contains 12 ringed four-leaf clovers conjoined around the six points of the apparent seal of Solomon, a symbol mostly recognized today as the Star of David. Although there was a large population of Jewish people living in the land in those days, this inherently Jewish emblem in a Catholic setting hints at the studies of alchemy and esoteric mysticism prominent among the rich and powerful during the Middle Ages.

Late in the night, as each pilgrim attempted to fall asleep, the bright fluorescent lights of the albergue didn't turn off. And there was no light switch. Downstairs at the front entrance, the check-in desk was empty. The Pilgrim went back upstairs and informed everyone that the front desk was abandoned and they would just have to sleep with the lights on. Several began to translate to their friends in German, Japanese, and French. Covering his eyes with a towel and drifting off to sleep, the Pilgrim wondered if perhaps they didn't normally turn the lights off at this place.

The next morning, the staff apologized profoundly. They had indeed forgotten to turn the lights off before heading home for the night.

Things happen on the Camino that tempt us to respond in anger. But we are learning to respond with humility.

The grand Santa Maria fountain sits in front of the massive cathedral. Along the Camino, one can find numerous fountains of various shapes and sizes. Most have water cascading and spurting from their spouts. Some of them are small, featuring drinkable water with a means to refill a thirsty pilgrim's water bottle or cup. It is a great delight to know that one or two of these fountains can actually be found to offer, not water, but wine – a little sip of which fortifies the weariest pilgrim's spirit!

We are reminded of the time Jesus himself turned water into wine. It was his first miracle. He was prompted by His Mother, a woman who, no doubt, was used to the inequality many women can sometimes endure. But Jesus obeyed her. He was attending a wedding when it happened. Well into the celebration, everyone was disappointed that the wine was running out. This was a shameful thing for the host. But then Jesus told the waiters to fill the jugs with water and serve them. They obeyed, even though they didn't know who He was. And to the surprise of everyone, the water poured out as wine. Moreover, it was the good wine that is usually served first, but this had been served late into the party. The host and the groom were honored!

This same Jesus accompanies us along the Camino de Santiago! He wants to celebrate with us on our journey too!

Camino Contemplation

Saint James knew that honor is a fruit of endurance, and it grows from roots of love.

God, in His kindness and generosity, desires to honor each of us. He honors us with something beautiful: never-ending life. Yes, our physical bodies will corrupt and one day pass away, but the essence of our very being will live on. He promises to give life to all who love God. We prove our love for God when we persevere through the hard trials of life. When we endure, we are saying yes to the way of God's Kingdom. His is a kingdom of light, not the path of darkness. We endure and prove that we love God, and then in turn, He honors us with life, which is one way He shows His love to us.

And it's not just a long and everlasting life; it's a life today that is abundant in hope, joy, and peace amidst the ever-present darkness.

Through our trials and tribulations, our faith grows stronger, and our connection with God deepens. As we walk the path that lies before us, let us remember that God is using it to teach us many things. He is using it to produce something good in us, something of great value that will last for an eternity.

Practical Application

Hardships will come, as certain as the rising sun. Yet, God promises to bless us with honor when we love Him and trust Him to bring us through these challenging times.

St. James Writes

James 1: 12 God honors those who endure hard trials, because God will reward them by making them live forever, as He has promised to do for all who love Him.

Prayer for the Peregrino

Dear Lord, thank you for the life eternal found in You. Thank you for the lessons I'm learning here on this Camino. I trust You this day to help me endure through life's trials. You alone are my Hope, my Light, and my Salvation.

In Christ's Name, Amen.

FIFTH DAY

> "Life is a pilgrimage, and unless love is attained, it remains a pilgrimage, never reaching anywhere."
>
> - Osho, Indian guru

The Path from Burgos to Hornillos del Camino

Just north, a two-day walk from Burgos, lies the town of Oña. It was there, in the Monastery of San Salvador, that sixteenth-century monk Pedro Ponce de León became the first teacher of the deaf when he developed the basis of a Sign Language alphabet. His pupils learned finger positions to spell words. His work opened the way for the Deaf community to learn about God. This method was then taken up to France, where it developed and became established as the basis for Deaf communication. Modern American Sign Language is based on the French Sign Language.

Leaving Burgos, the Pilgrim continued towards León, about a week's walk away. The challenging trek takes each pilgrim up and through the Meseta Central, the highland plateau that dominates the geography of Spain. The day's walk began later than anticipated. Early morning rain meant that the going was tough and slow, like thick molasses ebbing along in the cooler months. The sticky mud along the path proved to be an extra challenge for each pilgrim, especially those who were making their journey by peddling on a bicycle. Narrow and long, their tire grooves in the mud puddles filled with seeping water and left marks of this constant struggle.

The late morning brought bright and welcoming sunshine upon the land. The already verdant fields of grain were bursting with lush vegetation. The air, crisp and invigorating, filled the Pilgrim's lungs with life. Although his feet were sore, he walked forward with passionate pleasure. The path guided each pilgrim forward as they walked mostly at an easy gradual decline. Then, just before reaching the outskirts of Hornillos, the undulating land dropped into the valley, and the path of the Camino could be seen curving into the town. The view of the tiny village in the valley below provided extensive and breathtaking views of the Spanish countryside. Below lay a small, picturesque village, complete with a single cross atop the lone spire of the only church building for miles. As the pilgrims walked past, they could see that many of the walls of the cobblestone and brick buildings had potted plants decorating them.

Alas, late starts come with consequences. The only albergue in the village was already full, and there were about two dozen pilgrims still needing a place. With the next village too far away and a large group of weary pilgrims looking for shelter, the locals decided to open up their cold gymnasium, which had ample floor space for sleeping. A pile of muddy shoes guarded the entrance door. A sense of camaraderie was in the air. The village was small, and there was little to see. So, at an early hour that evening, all the pilgrims crawled into their sleeping bags on the hard, cold floor, hoping to get any amount of rest. This would be a rough night, probably one of the roughest on the Camino for the Pilgrim.

The Pilgrim's mind drifted to thoughts of home and family. As sleep came, aided by earplugs, thoughts of the journey became preeminent. Who were the people living in this village? When was the gymnasium built? What games do they play? What else have they built? What else is there to see?

The Camino de Santiago boasts thousands of historical

monuments, buildings, museums, and other incredibly interesting cultural curiosities. The majority of these are passed by, unknown to the pilgrim. If the purpose was not to complete the Camino, one could easily spend many hours learning and exploring the depths of each quiet village, mysterious town, and hidden hamlet.

Although pilgrims are not afforded the luxury of exploring every point of interest, they don't lose heart; for their quest is to continue to the end. Thankfully, for a brief moment along the way, no matter the state of urgency to continue onward, each pilgrim is invited to contemplate the divine and intrinsic beauty of the thing at hand, even if just in passing.

Many of these objects of interest, while good, can be distractions from the pilgrim's focus, which lies before and within. However, by ignoring the distractions, we are learning to better listen to the voice of God within our hearts, God's voice within the pages of the holy writ, and God's voice through the voices of friends and fellow pilgrims whom God graciously uses to speak to us.

Camino Contemplation

Following Christ on The Way of St. James is a journey through life, learning how to truly come alive.

Saint James defines sin simply as anything that causes complete death—the spiritual death of our souls. When we commit evil, it's almost tantamount to selling our souls to the devil. And every time we do this, the Evil One relentlessly accuses us, giving us a feeling of shameful condemnation. But Jesus comes and says that we are loved, accepted, and forgiven. He picks us up, dusts us off, and tells us to try again.

Sin traps us in a cycle of debt, which can only be repaid by blood —our blood—through what Saint James calls the final death, a spiritual death. He compassionately teaches us that only through Christ can we be saved from the shame and from the eternal repayment of the debt we owe.

Saint James invites us to accept the fact that Christ has already paid to free us from the judgment of final death. We are to ask for strength during times of temptation as we follow Christ on His Way that leads to life everlasting.

Practical Application

Sin is like a spiritual trap set to capture and kill the victim. Only Jesus can save us from this death.

St. James Writes

James 1: 13 *When we are tempted to sin, we must not think it is God who is tempting us, because God never wants to do evil, and he never tempts anyone to do evil.* **14** *But everyone wants to do evil, and so they do it, just as if they are falling into a trap.* **15** *After that, their evil thoughts lead them to commit sin, and this sin takes over their minds until it destroys them. Then, when evil desires come together, sin is born, which means the person commits sin and can only be forgiven by Jesus. And when sin produces its final result, death comes, both the death of the body and the death of the spirit, meaning the sinner is separated from God forever. Only Jesus can save us from this final death.*

Prayer for the Peregrino

Dear Lord, I thank you for making a way of salvation for me. I trust you in this. Today, I ask You for help to not fall into temptation. Lord, deliver me from evil. Help me to walk in Your way.

In Christ's Name, Amen.

SIXTH DAY

"If you are in a bad mood, go for a walk. If you are still in a bad mood, go for another walk."

- Hippocrates, Greek philosopher, Father of medicine

The Path from Hornillos del Camino to Castrojeriz

Rising upon the Camino de Santiago, the light of the sun burns away the obscuring fog, which has kissed the land with a gentle touch of mist. The solitude of the morning dew, bringing with it an air of mystery, guides each heart into a time of intentional contemplation.

Passing underneath the Arch of San Anton, where medical services were once offered to pilgrims along with bread left for any hungry passersby, the Pilgrim made his way steadily into —and through—the medieval town of Castrojeriz. Impressive castle ruins sleepily watched over the municipality from a strategic hilltop perch. The township below embraced the base of the hill like a crescent moon hugging the night sky. The trees that lined the path would have twinkled like stars with the early rays of the sun glistening off the early morning dew. But that had all evaporated many hours before the weary pilgrim would arrive. Regardless, each person walking was grateful for staggered moments of relief from the high sun.

Albergue de San Esteban was a fun and relaxing location to spend the night. Pleasant music gave the hostel a welcoming ambiance and complemented well with the muted colors of the paintings that adorned the walls. The lady running the hostel spoke the native tongue of the Pilgrim very well. He sensed that her magnetic kindness hid some unknown and painful memory. Quite early the next morning, as the pilgrims made their way back to the road, she was offering a substantial breakfast to anyone in need. Feeling grateful for her generosity and wanting God to heal the hidden pain, the Pilgrim said a prayer of blessing and protection over her, which she gratefully accepted.

Along the way, each pilgrim will pass a thin cross raised into the air. Standing in a solitary space on the right side of the road, it is the *Crucero Camino Frances*. It holds a small but significant connection with all the pilgrims that have passed by. In the vast mental barrenness of endless rolling hills of the northern Spanish countryside, here, and now, is another reminder of Christ, grounding the pilgrims to appreciate the moment of life that can be either enjoyed or taken for granted. For it is now in the journey that all initial excitement of everything new begins to wear away. Culture shock sets in. In the moment, if one is not careful, it can begin to feel like drudgery. There are no late-night parties like on Ibiza, no endless flavors to explore in the tapas of Andalucía, and no great monuments to behold. All seems ordinary.

Walking the Camino de Santiago can feel lonely at times. The Inner Plateau is great for planting fields of wheat and oat, but there is not much shade, especially between villages. Pilgrims start missing the fertile valleys and lush vineyards of earlier days. As the road passed roughly beneath the Pilgrim's tired feet, his mind drifted to something to occupy the dull, empty space. At times, we must push through an overwhelming feeling of loneliness to be able to keep our focus on Christ.

As pilgrims, we are learning to be okay with the slower pace of the wayfarer. Some like to listen to music or even an audiobook to occupy the endless hours. The Pilgrim tried that, and it simply wasn't sustainable.

When loneliness sets in, we must will ourselves to remember that although the pilgrim might walk by themselves, they never walk alone. For Christ is beside each one, and soon He will bring another pilgrim along the way to share a smile or a story over a cappuccino. Suddenly, and without surprise, the pilgrim may find themselves even longing for the emptiness of walking the path alone, where they are able to listen to the sound of silence, of nature, and of Christ within.

Camino Contemplation

In life, it's not enough to just be spiritual. Even demons are spiritual. Saint James teaches us that we must be spiritual in the way of Christ.

The Crucifix, found in almost every single cathedral and church building we pass by, is the symbol of Christ taking our place in the judgment of death. By Christ's death and resurrection from the dead, He offers us a new path of forgiveness, the only true path toward God. As Jesus Himself said, "I am the way, the truth, and the life. No one can come to God the Father unless he comes by the way of truth that I am showing you by my example and telling you about in person." (See John 14:6)

Walking alongside other pilgrims on the Camino de Santiago will likely become one of your most cherished memories. And that is a good gift. All good gifts come from God the Father in Heaven.

There is much darkness in the world, but Saint James teaches us that God gifts us with a light to illuminate our way and push back the darkness. Even when the darkness threatens to overcome us, we need to look for the light of Christ within ourselves. It is there, for He has given it to us to shine.

The light pushes back the darkness and also shows us the path to life. It's a double gift! As we walk on, let us trust Jesus Christ to give the gift of the Light of Himself and show us the way forward.

Practical Application

God loves to give really good gifts to His children. And the best gift is becoming alive within our spirits because of Jesus.

St. James Writes

James 1: 16 *My fellow believers whom I love, stop deceiving yourselves.* ***17*** *Every truly good and perfect gift comes from God the Father, who is in heaven. He is the true God who gives us light. God does not change like created things change, like shadows that appear and disappear. God never changes and He is always good!* ***18*** *God chose to give us spiritual life when we trusted in his true message. So now believers in Jesus have become the first people to have true spiritual life, which only Jesus can give.*

Prayer for the Peregrino

Dear God, thank you for being good. Thank you for sending Jesus Christ to light our way. Show me, I pray, Your path to life. I trust You to guide me along the way today.

In Christ's Name, Amen.

SEVENTH DAY

"If we find ourselves with a desire that nothing in this world can satisfy, the most probable explanation is that we were made for another world."

- C.S. Lewis, Literary scholar

The Path from Castrojeriz to Frómista

The seventh day of walking on the Camino de Santiago is sometimes ominously called the "Day of Pain." By now, blisters may have formed on the feet and on the hands of those using walking sticks. The entire body aches from the rigors of walking for miles every day. We massage our weary feet, hoping to regain the strength for the next day. Pilgrims are forced to attend to their wounds or risk infection. Thankfully, modern medicinal practices make it easy to take care of these small sores.

Those pilgrims who spend a few minutes each evening stretching out their back and leg muscles will find a lot of relief for the next day. In the mornings, the body has stiffened during the night's rest. A little vigorous massage of the calves and feet helps get the blood flowing. The sooner we set out on the path, the sooner our muscles will relax. We are sore but growing stronger each day as we persevere onward and forward.

Some time had passed since leaving Castrojeriz. Walking into a little shaded rest area for peregrinos, the Pilgrim looked ahead but could see only endless fields of grain. He was tempted to stop again. But if he stopped now, he knew he would lose momentum. "I must keep moving forward, one step at a time." Packing away the waterproof cloak that had been protection from rain and sleet in recent days, he thought kindly of his own father from whom it was gifted for the journey along the Camino.

Moving on outside Burgos, the Way of Saint James passes the old Hermitage of Saint Nicholas (San Nicolás de Puente Fitero). It's a small rectangular church building once inhabited by the Knights of Malta. A few months out of the year, it is open to small numbers of pilgrims who can spend the night here in this traditional shelter. It is famous for not having any electricity but boasts a warm embrace from the Italian confraternity that currently inhabits its thirteenth-century walls. These Benedictine monks live by the Codex Calixtinus and welcome the pilgrim as if the pilgrims themselves were Christ himself, or Saint James who had come to visit. And in the spirit of servitude, they offer the humbling ancient tradition of foot washing.

Immediately from here comes the bridge called Puente Fítero, also known as Itero Pass. This fine ashlar arched bridge boasts 11 arches over the wide Pisuerga River, making it one of the longest bridges on the Camino and strategically connecting the kingdoms of Castilla y León and Burgos. The half-moon arches of the bridge create an optically perfect circle shape when viewed from the perfect angle. Built sometime in the 800s, it was renovated 800 years later and stands to this day.

The Pisuerga River itself is over 175 miles in length. It begins its journey as meltwater from a mountain glacier in the Cantabrian Mountains in the north and flows in a southerly direction until it enters as a main tributary to the Duero River, which then flows through Portugal, emptying at last into the Atlantic Ocean.

Several more miles pass, and the Pilgrim arrives at the hostel in Frómista for the night. With great merriment, all the pilgrims eat and drink together at a restaurant that uses empty wine casks as decoration.

The industrial town of Frómista serves as a regional agricultural center, complete with a train track running through its outskirts. Life in this region proved to be challenging in the seventeenth century. Records show that there was a terrible famine due to locusts. A century later, after the town had declined, there was a resurgence, and a canal was built to help with irrigation. The Canal de Castilla was a lifesaver and still stands, giving every pilgrim a chance to walk over its life-giving path.

The Pilgrim paused to take in the serene beauty of the canal. He marveled at the ingenuity and resilience of those who had come before him. Reflecting on the powerful testament to human perseverance and adaptability that the canal represented, it had breathed life back into the region, transforming the once struggling town into a thriving agricultural hub.

As he stood there, he felt a profound connection to the generations of pilgrims who had walked this path before him, their footsteps echoing through time, and their stories intertwined with his own as they shared this ancient and sacred journey.

Camino Contemplation

Saint James, in his writings, emphasizes the importance of humility. He advises us to listen first, and then speak. As much as we might desire to express and explain ourselves, doing so can often prove fruitless.

Anger is a worldly darkness that deceives us into selfish pride, making us believe that we are without flaws. Whether or not we are correct in our argument is beside the point; that is not the true focus. By exercising self-control and refraining from arguing or becoming angry with a person or situation, we cultivate the fruit of a life rooted in Christ.

Through practicing humility, we gain the ability to focus our attention on Christ, whose Holy Spirit guides us along our journey. How deeply do you wish to follow the way of Jesus? Are you willing to forsake your pride and ego, allowing humility to become the cloak you wear?

Practical Application

The next time someone seeks to argue with you, allow yourself to be humbled by letting them prevail, just as Christ remained silent before his accusers. This act of humility will help you draw closer to Christ and grow in your spiritual journey.

St. James Writes

James 1: 19 *My fellow believers whom I love, you know that every one of you should be eager to pay attention to God's true message. You should not quickly speak your own thoughts, nor quickly get angry,* **20** *because when we get angry we cannot do the righteous things that God wants us to do.*

Prayer for the Peregrino

Dear Lord, thank you for teaching me humility. Forgive me for not always speaking truth. Today I ask that You help me to say "no" to anger and to speak only the words that are pleasing in Your sight. Thank you for helping me along the way.

In Christ's Name, Amen.

EIGHTH DAY

"It's not about the shoes, it's what you do in them."

- Michael Jordan, US basketball player

The Path from Frómista to Carrión de los Condes

The pilgrims remain deep in the territory of Castile and León, traversing the high and arid land of the *Meseta Central*. They will not enter the mountainous region for many days until they begin to leave Castile and León and journey into Galicia. For now, vast expanses of cultivated farmland stretch as far as the eye can see. Some pilgrims, having glimpsed the path ahead, have opted to take the bus back in Burgos to skip this part of the Camino and proceed directly to Leon. There is not much to explore along the way. Thankfully, the green and yellow sunflower fields make this monotonous stretch easier to endure, but only when in bloom.

It was only a few days into the journey on the Camino de Santiago that the Pilgrim encountered a powerful and dark seductress. She is a force that each pilgrim must face at some point along the way. Her siren call aims to entice each pilgrim to abandon their journey along the Camino.

For almost a week, the Pilgrim had walked strong. But as the miles accumulated, his shoes wore out, quite literally. The shoes had been a gift from his brother. However, the Pilgrim was oblivious to the fact that these flat shoes were not designed for long-distance walking. The foot pain became so excruciating that he fell behind, eventually coming to a complete halt in a small town whose name he never learned. Grimacing involuntarily, the Pilgrim leaned in agony against a stone wall, feeling discouraged. Was this what being left behind felt like with his fellow pilgrims far ahead of him? It seemed as though no other pilgrims had passed by for hours.

Deciding that now would be a good time to escape the many challenges of the Camino, the Pilgrim decided to give up and retreat to the comforts of home. He turned back to abandon the journey. This was it. He was done. Taking steps in the direction from which he had come, the pain remained unabated. The siren call was loud and pervasive, drawing him with apathy into the way he knew he should not follow. She lured his weary heart with the empty promise of pain-free comfort. Yet he was still in pain on the path back.

The Pilgrim felt torn in two. To retreat was easy. To continue meant weeks more of unbearable pain. Deciding to lie down in a small abandoned clearing, the Pilgrim closed his eyes in surrender, wishing the end of the world upon himself.

"God, please, help me!" He whispered in final desperation.

Suddenly, the Pilgrim realized that the boisterous call of the siren of solace was not the only beckoning voice. There was another. This one was a still, small voice urging the Pilgrim forward to complete this sacred journey. The Pilgrim could not quit, not here, not now. But the thought of continuing under the weight of suffering crushed his fragile spirit. Praying for divine assistance, the Pilgrim resolved to keep moving forward towards the finish line.

There was no sudden burst of energy, no apparition of clarity, no particular divine revelation. Only sheer will and a nod of approval from God, saying this was the path he should follow. And he walked slowly. But he was moving forward.

Hours later, as the sun was setting, he reached Carrión de los

Condes. To his relief, he happened upon a small shop selling new footwear to pilgrims. After having walked for days through the wilderness of the high Inner Plateau without seeing so much as a modern coffee shop or ATM, this was an incredible find. Although the new walking shoes weren't expensive, the cost would consume the remainder of what little savings he had left. Relenting, the Pilgrim purchased the shoes and joined the others for dinner with a renewed enthusiasm.

The Pilgrim could have turned back, abandoning his quest. But having fought his way forward in obedience to the voice of Christ within, there was a miraculous provision in his time of greatest need. These shoes were truly a good gift from God.

Camino Contemplation

Saint James implores us to cease doing evil and begin doing good. This is not merely about following rules for their own sake; it is about obedience to the voice of Christ within our hearts. His voice illuminates our path and guides us toward life. Saint James understands that evil deafens us to the voice of Christ.

Merely listening to God's Word is insufficient to generate life; we must apply the wisdom by adhering to and obeying what God says. Acting on what we hear helps us remember what was said and prepares us to receive the good gifts of life from God the Father. But we must listen, truly listen.

Let us resolve in our hearts not just to hear the voice but to obey the voice of Christ within.

Practical Application

You are free to do whatever you want. However, anything without God leads to spiritual bondage. God sets us free and grants us even greater freedom when we listen to Him. He then shows us what to do and allows us to make the choice ourselves. With obedience comes God's blessings and favor.

St. James Writes

James 1: 21 *So stop doing all kinds of evil, and humbly accept the message that God planted in your inner beings, because he is able to save you if you accept his message.* ***22*** *Do what God commands in his message. Do not only listen to it, because people who only listen to it and do not obey it think wrongly that God will save them.* ***23*** *Some people hear God's message but do not do what it says. They are like someone who looks at his face in a mirror.* ***24*** *Although he looks at himself, he goes away from the mirror and immediately forgets what he looks like.* ***25*** *But other people look closely at God's message, which is perfect and which sets people free to voluntarily do what God* wants them to do. And if they continue to examine God's message and do not just hear it and then forget it, but do what God tells them to do, God will bless them because of what they do.

Prayer for the Peregrino
Dear Lord, thank you for speaking to me. Today, I humbly ask You to help me listen to You and block out the voice of deception. My heart's desire is to follow You. Thank you for helping me along the way.

In Christ's Name, Amen.

NINTH DAY

> "All of us are on a journey of the heart, and so this external walking, this external journeying, is really a symbol of us moving towards God."
>
> - Bishop Hying, *Santiago, the Camino Within*

The Path from Carrión de los Condes to Terradillos de los Templarios

After purchasing the new shoes, the next morning the Pilgrim set out on the trail, fully expectant that they would do what they were designed to do. He left the old ones behind and pressed forward towards what lay ahead. The going was brisk, sunny, and exciting. The world changed since he had put on the new footwear. The difference was absolutely astounding. With proper footwear, finishing the Camino was possible.

Walking the countryside path towards Terradillos, he found he was keeping pace with the fastest pilgrim. Passing a field of rolled hay bales, the two of them got lost and went the wrong way. After consulting a pocket map and realizing their mistake, they backtracked, cut across a field of flowers, and found the right path. They eventually made it to their destination before the rest of their group of pilgrims arrived.

The shoes were a gift. The Pilgrim was grateful for the strength to keep moving forward. The little miracles and small victories help encourage us pilgrims as we make our way towards the goal. Yes, making a bad decision can happen, and we can find ourselves lost. But, we can always backtrack and find our way again.

The pilgrims would pass through the pretty little villages of Calzadilla de la Cueza and Ledigos, each with fewer than 100 inhabitants. The local church building in Ledigos is dedicated to Saint James. In Calzadilla de la Cueza, the population might even double from 50 in the busy months of the year just from the passing pilgrims who might want to stay with them.

In this place, life seems to be challenging, but also simple. The concerns of massive urban areas don't bother the small village locals. The people in the villages work to support the local farms, pray for rain for their crops, and take pride in being the hard workers they are.

At *Los Templarios Albergue*, the pilgrims were treated well and sat down to a homemade dinner of *paella*, the famous Spanish dish made of a wide variety of seafood, meat, and rice seasoned with bright saffron and aromatic spices. It is traditionally cooked in a wide and shallow dish. The way to a man's heart is through his stomach, or so the saying goes. As a bachelor at the time, the Pilgrim decided that if the young lady who had cooked the delicious food wanted him to stay forever, he would have left everything and stayed.

But alas, it was not meant to be. True love would be found elsewhere; and she would be worth the wait!

The locals at Terradillos de los Templarios have a legend. They believe that the last of the Templars buried the famous hen that laid the golden eggs nearby their little village. Since this was a small Knights Templar outpost of little importance, no one would think to look for it here. And so they keep this secret safe from the world.

Camino Contemplation

It is no secret that much of the world seems godless. Unholy vices such as greed, gossip, and gluttony, along with sexual perversions, abound. Many people sense this darkness and spiritual disconnect. In response, they try to emphasize a pious way of life to reconnect with the Living God. However, most of these attempts are misguided, as they do not follow God's leading.

It can be easy to be distracted by the many *antichrist* voices that try to deceive us into believing a lie mixed with truth. But true followers of Christ are freed from this deception, as they are guided by the Truth of His Spirit.

Saint James helps to bring clarity to the chaos, teaching us that we can express our worship of God and our adoration for Him in many ways, for not all expressions are inherently bad. However, he warns that our actions can be worthless if we do not obey what God has said. At the foundation of all that is holy in this world, the best way to express our faith in Christ is to speak wisely, provide for the needs of both widows and orphans who can never repay us, and strive to keep ourselves unblemished by the things of the world that would leave a mark of darkness on us. Christ helps us in all things. All temptations are common among humankind, so there is no shame in asking God for help. We have all been there before.

When we live in pursuit of that which leads to death and still try to offer our expressions of worship to God, our worship becomes futile. How can clean water and dirty water flow from the same source?

When we live in pursuit of Christ, walk in obedience in both thought and deed, and learn to love others well, we can stand approved before God the Father.

Let us resolve to speak wisely, act wisely, and do something to help the fatherless and widows of the world, no matter where we go.

Practical Application

What we say and what we do matters. The only acceptable religion to God comprises three basic characteristics: helping the vulnerable orphans and widows, keeping oneself unpolluted from the darkness in the world, and controlling what we say.

St. James Writes

James 1: 26 *Some people think that they worship God rightly, but they habitually speak evil talk. Those people are wrong in thinking that they worship God rightly. The fact is that they worship God in vain.* **27** *One of the things that God has told us to do is to take care of orphans and widows who suffer hardship. Those who do that, and who do not think or act immorally like those who do not obey God, truly worship God, who is our Father, and God approves of them.*

Prayer for the Peregrino

Dear Lord, thank you for giving me the chance to love and worship You in my thoughts and actions. I ask, dear Lord, that You would help me to worship You by obeying all that You have commanded us. I know that it is for my good, even if I don't always understand why.

In Christ's Name, Amen.

TENTH DAY

> "Lord…you have made us for yourself, and our heart is restless until it rests in you."
>
> - St. Augustine of Hippo, fifth-century Christian saint

The Path from Terradillos to El Burgo Raneros

The walk from Terradillos to El Burgo Raneros was long. There is a quaint village called Moratinos with a famous hill named "El Castillo de Moratinos." This hill is studded with little hobbit-like entrances to caves used for storing and preserving wine by the local families.

Further down the road is a small monument marking the border with the province of León.

Then just a bit further, the geographical halfway mark between Roncesvalles and Santiago de Compostela is found in front of a small thirteenth-century hermitage made in the Mudéjar style just before Sahagún. One must take a small detour off the main path, cross over the bridge spanning the modest Valderaduey River to reach it. The marker is a large stone monument composed of two concrete statues. One is of a knight with a sword in his right hand and orders to protect in his left. The second one is a Benedictine monk standing over a bushel of wheat and a basket of bread and fruit. In his right hand, he holds a sickle over the wheat, and in his left, he grasps a Bible with the words Ora et Labora, a poignant reminder to work and pray. The statues face each other as pilgrims walk between them to continue from this place without backtracking.

Pilgrims will pass through, or may stay, in Sahagún. It is here that the beautifully intricate Mudéjar style of art and architecture first appeared. This style is a mixture of Gothic and Islamic design.

Muslim conquerors under the eighth-century Umayyad Caliphate had conquered most of the Iberian Peninsula, renaming it Al-Andalus. They brought with them not only a new religion but also a unique form of arts and architecture. Sahagún was one of the northernmost outposts in this Al-Andalus.

During the eleventh through fifteenth centuries, the Christians went on a quest to reconquer the lands and began moving back into the settlements abandoned by the exiled Moors. With the expulsion of these Muslims from the Iberian Peninsula by the Catholic Church during the Middle Ages, inevitably some stayed and didn't convert. Instead, they were tolerated and allowed to live amongst the people. Those who stayed and their artistic designs were called Mudéjar.

The people in Sahagún appreciated the old Moorish designs, took the Mudéjar design further, and adopted this arabesque style into their own art and architecture. A new sort of hybrid was then created that pulled elements from both Islamic and Christian techniques. It is a richly ornate decoration style defined by components of intricate geometric motifs, elegant vegetal shapes, and stylized pseudo-Kufic calligraphy that resembles Arab lettering but doesn't actually mean anything.

Back on the Camino, by the time the Pilgrim arrived in El Burgo Raneros with the group, all the hostels were full except one which had only six beds available. With such a large group in need, there was no way the lady of the house was going to fit the dozen weary pilgrims into her hostel. The remaining six pilgrims would occupy the floor in her own home for the night.

Mentally and physically exhausted, the Pilgrim watched with

sadness as other peregrinos passed through the little town where there was no room. Though late in the day as it was, they could not rest until they found shelter, which was in the next town over, still an hour's walk away.

The Pilgrim thought about the journey of the pregnant Virgin Mary and her soon-to-be husband, Joseph. They themselves had no doubt walked through many small villages like this one without finding a place to rest. Her weary body, tired from a day's ride on a donkey and full of Life within, would find room only in a humble farm stable. But from that humbling experience, the Savior of the world would be born.

Questions crossed the Pilgrim's mind as more pilgrims had to be turned away. Would the innkeepers and *hosteliers* have made room for Mary and Joseph if they had just known? Did they think these pilgrims from afar were poor and unimportant? Would they have treated them differently if they were dressed like royalty or had known they were pregnant with the King?

Camino Contemplation

Saint James enlightens us with a principal teaching of *equality in judgment*.

Christ honors those who walk in the path of light that He reveals along the way. He desires to approve of everyone, but not everyone walks in obedience. Some walk in disobedience by neglecting the poor, while at the same time honoring the rich. This is dishonorable. Saint James warns us not to dishonor the poor.

As we walk the Camino, let us endeavor to show equality in judgment by loving and considering everyone better than ourselves. For in the face of a stranger, we see the reflection of Christ.

Practical Application

The Golden Rule: Do unto others as you would want them to do to you. God resists the proud but gives grace to the humble.

St. James Writes

James 2: 1 *My brothers and sisters, because you trust our Lord Jesus Christ, the one who is greater than anything, stop honoring some people more than others.* **2** *For example, suppose that a person who wears gold rings and fine clothes enters your meeting place. Then suppose that a poor person who wears shabby clothes also comes in.* **3** *And suppose that you show special attention to the one dressed in fine clothes by saying, "Please sit here in this nice seat!" and you say to the poor one, "You stand over there or sit on the floor!"* **4** *You have then judged one another for wrong reasons.*

5 *Listen to me, my brothers and sisters whom I love. God has chosen poor people who seem to have nothing of value, to trust in him very much. So he will give them great things when he rules everyone everywhere. This is what he has promised to do for everyone who loves him.*

6 *But you dishonor the poor people. Think about it! It is the rich people, not the poor people, who are causing you to suffer! It is the rich people who forcibly take you to court to accuse you in front of judges!* **7** *And they are the ones who speak evil against the Lord Jesus Christ, the one who is worthy of praise, to whom you belong!* **8** *Jesus our King has commanded you in the Scriptures that each of you must love other people like you love yourself. If you love others, you do what is right.* **9** *But if you honor some people more than others, you are doing wrong. And because you do not do what God commanded us to do, he condemns you because you disobey his laws.*

Prayer for the Peregrino

Dear Lord, thank you for guiding me along the way. Help me to show no partiality toward anyone but to honor and love all with the love and honor that You have shown me. Thank you for teaching me humility.

In Christ's Name, Amen.

ELEVENTH DAY

"As the 'blessed ones,' we can walk through this world and offer blessings."

- Henry Nouwen, Dutch Catholic priest and theologian

The Path from El Burgo Raneros to Mansilla de las Mulas

Like much of this part of the Camino, the walk from El Burgo Raneros to Mansilla de las Mulas can feel pretty lonely and dull, except for the little villages of Villamarco and Reliegos to break up the monotony. One is obliged to press on, step by step. Black hawks soar overhead, looking for a tasty morsel in the windswept fields of grain. The Merino sheep, originally introduced from North Africa in the early Middle Ages, have been taken further north into the cooler mountains for the summer while the wheat grows here. Now, just frogs and lizards abound, although hidden in the cooler crevices and shadows of bushes.

Walking in a northerly course up towards León, pilgrims pass another cross. It is a welcomed reprieve from the solitude of the road and brings with it a sense of security. Before the traditional yellow arrow that is the standard today, pilgrims of yore relied on these raised crosses to find their way.

Additionally, there are extra pilgrim rest areas to aid in breaking up the rather dull part of the path. Because the villages are few, pilgrims bring extra water and food to sustain the long walk through the Meseta. Few rivers flow through the land, and consequently, there are few trees large enough to provide much shade until reaching the fertile town of Mansilla de las Mulas. In recent years, the local government has planted a row of trees along the path that help provide shade for the grateful pilgrims.

The cool mountains are still several days away. Pilgrims long for relief from the arid flatland of the Meseta. Protruding in the distance, the mountain peaks are beginning to appear. For now, they might as well be mirages. It would be easy to give up if it were not for the simple joy of being humble pilgrims on a journey. Almost a few weeks have passed since the pilgrims started at the beginning, and there is still much more to walk. Each pilgrim has come so far. Now is not the time to give up. Unfortunately, for some, they are forced to retire early from their quest due to severe injuries, like tendinitis, as a result of walking too much. And this begs the question: Perhaps we are pushing ourselves unnecessarily to complete the Camino in under 40 days.

The Pilgrim himself longs to have had the chance to make this pilgrimage moving town to town, one day at a time, and remaining in those places that are particularly interesting and special. That trip would take many months, but the wear on the body would be manageable, and the journey fathomless.

Mansilla de las Mulas is a nice-sized town of around 2,000 inhabitants. There is an ethnographic museum showcasing the Leonese history, culture, and language.

Along the way, the Pilgrim observed that even the smallest villages in Spain are made of façades. Here was no exception. However, instead of hiding an unpleasant view, they more often than not serve as doorways to a world of private beauty, known only to those who enter. Façades help provide a sort of built-in security for the inner inhabitants who have ample open space in their courtyards and walkways.

The pilgrim's hostel in Mansilla de las Mulas also had this courtyard. It was plastered with a vibrant yet mellow yellow.

On the walls hung dozens of red-clay pots with flowers bursting in purples, reds, and pinks, blooming all around. At eventide, the wine flowed, and echoes of laughter rang out as the weary pilgrims, barefoot or sandaled, rejoiced in the inner beauty of this place. As the sun set, a guitar strummed, and they sang folk songs until their eyelids drooped heavily, and one by one, they retired to their bunks.

Yes, the Camino is demanding on the body, but the mind and the soul are set free to be delighted by the simple beauties of life.

Camino Contemplation

Saint James knew the painful beauty of obedience. When we were young, we had to learn to blindly obey our parents. They gave us instructions and rules that we didn't think about. Later in life, we began to question why. We were forced to eat vegetables as children because, as immature youngsters, we did not yet have a taste or appreciation for eating healthily.

We thought our parents were being hard on us, but eating vegetables for the sake of eating vegetables just because we were told to was not the point. It was really about our health and longevity. And as children mature, they begin to understand the deeper reality of their parents' insistence on eating the healthy food.

One's spiritual life reflects the rhythm of life in the natural. Your human life began at conception, you were born as an infant, grew into a child, and then, through many trials and tribulations, lessons and experiences, you have grown into maturity. It has been a gradual process.

Saint James points us to a deeper reality of the divine edicts. There are many of them, and we don't often fully understand at first why God would give such arbitrary rules. But as we mature, we begin to understand why.

Being guilty of disobedience of God's law is not just about being guilty of God's law. It's really about our spiritual health and longevity. It's about having a good relationship with our Heavenly Father and growing up into spiritual maturity.

The wisdom of Saint James invites us into greater levels of this maturity and, ultimately, deeper intimacy with Jesus Christ.

As we walk the Camino, let us purpose to trust that God is setting certain boundaries for our own good, even if we don't fully understand the reason for them.

Practical Application

If you break one commandment, you are guilty of breaking all God's laws. Therefore, we must rely fully on God for His grace and mercy.

St. James Writes

James 2: 10 *Those who disobey only one of God's laws, even if they obey all his other laws, God considers to be as guilty as anyone who has disobeyed all of his laws.* **11** *For example, God said, "Do not commit adultery," but he also said, "Do not murder anyone." So if you do not commit adultery but you murder someone, you have become a person who disobeys God's laws.*

Prayer for the Peregrino

Dear Lord, I know that I have disobeyed Your laws. Please forgive me. Help me to grow into maturity in You and deeper intimacy with Your presence. Thank you for guiding me along the way.

In Christ's Name, Amen.

TWELFTH DAY

"For pilgrims walking…every footfall is doubled, landing at once on the actual road and also on the path of faith."

- Robert Macfarlane, British nature and travel writer

The Path from Mansilla de las Mulas to León

Outside Mansilla, the road passes underfoot. Soon, a bridge with eight arches spanning the impressive Esla River appears. Icy waters born in the snowcaps of the Cantabrian Mountain range contribute collective droplets to the Duero River. From here, these main tributary waters eventually empty into the Atlantic Ocean some 500 miles later.

The Iberian Peninsula had been under the control of the Roman Empire when Saint James made his journey there and established Christianity. By the fourth century, the Roman Empire had adopted what had evolved into Catholicism, and it spread even further in the peninsula. The Roman rule was dissolved in 472 by the conquering of a pagan Germanic people called the Visigoths, who became Christianized.

Enter the early Medieval Age. This Kingdom of the Goths enjoyed dominion for almost 240 years. In the year 711, North African Muslims under the Umayyad dynasty, called Moors, attacked and conquered most of the Visigoth kingdoms in the Iberian Peninsula, except for a sliver of land in the mountains in the far north, including a land called Asturias.

About ten years after the conquest by the Moors, a nobleman

named Pelagius (Pelayo) became king of the northern Kingdom of Asturias after he had gathered together a band of mountain dwellers, resisted the Muslim domination, and won the decisive *Battle of Covadonga*. This would prove to be the beginning of the 700-year-long *Reconquista*, during which the Moors would continue to attack.

The third king of Asturias, Alfonso I (739 – 757), depopulated a vast tract of the Meseta to provide a no man's land known as the *Desert of the Duero*. It acted as a buffer zone to deter the would-be attackers from coming back, as there was nobody to rule over. People were only permitted to reside in designated cities, although a few did live outside these cities during this time.

It was during the reign of Alfonso II (760 – 842) that the mysterious sepulcher of Saint James would be discovered in a forest in Galicia. Alfonso II would become the first pilgrim to the shrine of Saint James.

Then the time came to repopulate the largely uninhabited land of the "deserted" Duero basin in the ninth century. The initial resettlement was completed by the year 910 when the kingdom was divided amongst the three great nephews of Alfonso I of Asturias. The resettlement of the Desert of the Duero is now called the *Repoblación*, a term also referring to the art and architecture of those Christians who lived under Christian rule but still built and designed in the Mozarabic fashion.

Mozárab is the modern term now used to refer to those Christians in Iberia under Moorish rule, the form of art and architecture of those same Christians, as well as their language.

Just to the north of Mansilla de las Mulas is a monastery that was built just after the time of the Repoblación. It features the Mozárabic (Repoblación) design, including the distinctive Moorish horseshoe arch, one of the arabesque elements inspired by Islamic architecture prominent in the southern parts of the Iberian Peninsula. While this style is not often seen in Christian architecture, this particular monastery is considered to be one of the best-preserved monasteries of its kind in Spain.

It is this *Desert of the Duero* that the pilgrims of today walk through on their way to Santiago de Compostela.

On the Camino, under the scourge of the summer sun, thistles and lavender grow in solidarity with the land. It's as if they are ardently daring the heat to beat them down and wither. "Come, do your worst!" they scream in swaying silence. Yet, here they grow summer after summer, year after year, age after age.

Walking over a large blue pedestrian bridge with a good view of the big city, a fellow from Brazil passed the Pilgrim an agate-blue stone and a rustic orange stone, both mechanically polished. This other pilgrim explained that each one must bring a stone from their country to leave at a designated point in the coming days ahead. Not having known this before nor having his own stones, the Pilgrim was grateful to receive the little pebbles from Brazil. Further down the road, another ancient bridge called Castro leads each pilgrim into the old Jewish quarter on the outskirts of the old city.

Teeming with a population of over one million, León will be the last major city before reaching Santiago de Compostela, still a couple of weeks away. The iconic cathedral in León is known for the massive amounts of stained glass that, some say, threatens to compromise its structural integrity.

Day by day, the mountains in the Northwest draw even closer. Soon in the westward trek, each pilgrim will have to trudge upward and over these mountains leading towards Compostela. But for tonight, the Pilgrim is in León.

Camino Contemplation

Saint James writes about judgment and the Law of Liberty. This powerful reality is more than a decree for simple morality. It is the foundation of virtue, a tool with which mercy serves as the cornerstone. The Law of Liberty goes deeper than mere freedom. Freedom is external and can be taken by external forces. In all cultures around the world, governments and politicians may eventually take away personal freedoms, but we are still free to choose to love our neighbor, trust God, and reject the temptation of fear.

Christ on the Cross said, "Father, forgive them, for they do not know what they are doing." Jesus exemplified the Law of Liberty. They were killing Him, and yet He chose to pray words of blessing over them.

Liberty is an inner place of existential freedom, the freedom of self, our heart, and our conscience. No matter what happens in the world, this inner freedom can never be taken, only surrendered. We may be oppressed from every side, but we are not crushed. Christ was crushed in our place. The forces of darkness may attack and persecute followers of the Way of Christ, as they always have, but we are not abandoned. Jesus gives us the strength to press on as we abide in Him.

God is the ultimate judge. But He is merciful. He forgives when He has the power to punish. He wants us to do the same! In embracing this mercy and extending it to others, we deepen our faith.

Practical Application

Mercy triumphs over judgment!

St. James Writes

James 2: 12 *So speak and obey as those who are about to be judged by the law of liberty.* **13** *For judgment comes without mercy to those who have shown no mercy. Mercy triumphs over judgment!*

Prayer for the Peregrino

Dear Lord, thank you for showing me mercy. Give me strength to walk in love toward my neighbor. I ask You to help me speak and obey You and to choose Your virtuous path. Thank you for giving me Your strength.

In Christ's Name, Amen.

THIRTEENTH DAY

"Everywhere is within walking distance if you have the time."

- Steven Wright, American comedian

The Path from León to San Martín del Camino

The Moorish cartographer Idrisi, in the year 1150, described the city of León as "one of the most major and prosperous cities of Castilla, whose inhabitants, by nature warlike, noble, and prudent, dedicated themselves to commerce and industry, especially the raising of cattle." (Gitlitz, Davidson 1999, pg. 246)

León, originally built to guard ancient Galician gold mines and founded in the same year as the fall of Jerusalem, boasts 2000 years of history within its ancient Roman fortifications. León had become an anchor point for Christianity about two centuries before its establishment as the legal religion of the Roman Empire.

On the outskirts of the city, there is an area with houses that appear as if built out of a hill, topped with dirt and grass. These structures are actually granaries, not the hobbit homes the Pilgrim had hoped they would be.

Beyond that, more fields. These lands have witnessed countless battles—Barbarians fighting Christians, who in turn defended their land from the invading Moors. Later, Napoleon's troops would push into this area in the early nineteenth century. The Pilgrim wonders, why so much violence, so much bloodshed?

For most of the day, the Pilgrim walks solo, lost in thought. His mind wanders with the butterflies that flutter past, grappling with existential questions. What is the point of this journey? He is working hard to walk a new path, but what good will come from this? Is it even worth it? Desperation permeates his mind, his spirit sinking into the depths of despair.

After spending a few hours passing under the shaded areas of poplar and cedar pine trees, he decides to stop in a small town just short of Hospital de Órbigo, a more popular stop along the way.

This place, San Martín del Camino, is a simple, quiet little haven with a network of canals in its surrounding fields of wheat. The canals have replaced the old wells once pumped by animals. This new technology has allowed the locals to produce additional crops of corn and potatoes.

Nesting storks have built multiple nests atop many of the town's high points. These storks return to the same nests in early springtime, after wintering in Africa.

Later in the evening, while sitting down to another meal of paella, the Pilgrim sips from his wine glass and then slips into his bunk. Under the weight of despair and the covers, he silently prays. Like the Israelites of old, the Pilgrim asks, "God, why did you bring me to this desolate area?" The Pilgrim is tired of fighting the good fight. Is he the only one who must fight despair?

Inundated by the echoes of past battles and of the present ones, the Pilgrim confronts his own spiritual struggles. Amidst uncertainty and the labyrinth of doubt, he finds solace in the knowledge that he need not laboriously pursue meaning by walking the Camino as meaning is already gifted by God. In the same way, he need not work for salvation, for Jesus has already gifted it. Sleep comes swiftly as this profound realization invigorates his spirit and rekindles his purpose.

Tomorrow will be another day. Fewer than 200 miles remain, and the allure of the distant mountains that draw closer continues to propel him forward on the path.

Camino Contemplation

Saint James was intimately familiar with the passion of Christ. He was a friend of Jesus while He walked this earth. Jesus shed real tears during the Crucifixion, and Saint James was passionate about sharing this passion of Christ with others.

Certainly, he encountered people who claimed to have faith in Jesus Christ but did nothing externally to demonstrate their faith. Saint James boldly called out this hypocrisy and wrote a challenge for us pilgrims that remains applicable today.

He observed that having genuine faith in Christ compels one to do good deeds, and more so, that these things would naturally (supernaturally) flow out of the goodness of the Light of Christ within. Disciples of Christ don't perform good deeds because they're "supposed to"; rather, good works flow naturally from a heart full of real faith, like a fresh water flows out of a spring. They can't help but do good deeds.

Today, we are challenged to walk the path of Saint James and give out of the goodness of our hearts. Not because we are inherently good, but because Christ, in His good mercy, has made us virtuous through His Passion on the Cross. Remember, it's less about merely sharing the theology of your faith and more about sharing and showing the reality of your faith by doing good works. In fact, God Himself demonstrated His love for us in that while we were still in our sin, Christ died for us (See Romans 5:8).

Let your faith inspire you to serve others, deepen your relationship with God, and ultimately, become a living testimony of His love and mercy.

Practical Application

Don't work for salvation. Work because Christ has already gifted you salvation!

St. James Writes

James 2: 14 *What good is it, my brothers, if someone say he has faith, but he has no works? Can that faith save him?* **15** *If a brother or sister is in need of clothes and daily food,* **16** *and one of you says to them, "Go in peace, be warmed and eat well," but you do not give them the things necessary for the body, what good is that?* **17** *In the same way faith by itself, if it does not have works, is dead.* **18** *Yet someone will say, "You have faith, and I have works." Show me your faith without works, and I will show you my faith by my works.*

Prayer for the Peregrino

Dear Lord, thank you for showing me Your path of virtue. I humbly ask You to help me demonstrate my faith in You by loving and serving those whose path I cross. And may the words I share about You reflect truthfully in my life. Thank you for demonstrating Your love for me on the Cross.

In Christ's Name, Amen.

FOURTEENTH DAY

"One road leads home and a thousand roads lead into the wilderness."

- C.S. Lewis

The Path from San Martín del Camino to Astorga

Emerging from San Martín, pilgrims enter the town of Hospital de Órbigo. Approaching the quaint town of only a thousand residents, they cross over an impressive thirteenth century Gothic-style bridge with 19 arches—one of the most iconic Roman bridges. Due to flooding and wars, some portions of the bridge have been rebuilt as recently as the nineteenth century.

This is no ordinary bridge, however. It's a portal to both the future and the past. The bridge, nicknamed the "passage of honor", is tied to a quixotic story from 1434. As the world transitioned from the Middle Ages into the Renaissance, chivalry and honor had not yet faded.

A knight, smitten by a fair maiden whose heart he could not win, resolved to prove his love by fighting for it in the best way he knew how: by holding a jousting tournament. For a few weeks during that Jacobean Holy Year, challengers from all over crossed the 19 arches of the *Passo Honroso* to duel the fiery knight in shining armor.

After 300 lances from his opponents had been shattered, he declared himself the reigning champion, capturing the fair maiden's heart—or perhaps he let go of his desire and moved on; history remains unclear. Either way, in honor of his victory, he became another pilgrim and journeyed to Santiago de Compostela to give thanks.

The pilgrims are now approaching the Montes de León with the Cantabrian Range to the north and the passage through the Inner Plateau nearing its end. Though monuments may be sparse, the dramatic scenery unfolding along the way is worth every step. Pilgrims will encounter more chestnut trees, oak trees, and patches of yellow-flowered broom shrubs as well as purple-flowered heather, which may or may not be in bloom, depending on the time of year.

One of the infamous ancient Roman roads used for commercial purposes is the Via de la Plata. Although *plata* is the Spanish word for silver, they say that silver was never traded along this route, at least not in significant quantities. It's more likely a corruption of the Arabic word *al-balat*, meaning "the paved road." But such is the evolution of language. Some pilgrims choose to walk this route to Santiago de Compostela.

The Via de la Plata begins in southern Spain, in Andalusia, where the Moors once reigned. This route runs parallel to the Portuguese border, eventually converging in the city of Astorga, where the Pilgrim will rest for the night—just as Saint Francis of Assisi did in this very town on his own pilgrimage in 1214.

Astorga is the last significant township before the upward climb into the Montes de León. As such, it naturally became popular among both pilgrims and merchants. It is an ideal place to resupply and gather strength before the arduous journey up into the mountains, serving as a natural spot for travelers to rest and rejuvenate while heading westward.

A chocolate museum that is consistently bustling with patrons, except when closed, invites pilgrims to explore the fascinating world of chocolate, from cacao bean to chocolate bar, and learn about the traditions of hand-making it as well as modern machinery. Spanish conquistador Hernán Cortés could never have fathomed the impact that the cacao bean would have on the world. In 1528, he brought a sample from his travels to the New World back to Astorga, where it was well received. This unwittingly established Astorga as the birthplace of chocolate for the whole of Europe! It is here that the rich legacy of the cacao bean and its history endures to this day.

The area also holds another significant story. It is believed that an actual relic of the wooden Cross upon which Christ died was once kept within the city. When the Moors invaded in the eighth century, the relic was safeguarded in a secret location a few hours north of Astorga. Today, this artifact resides in the nearby *Santo Toribio de Liébana* monastery.

Camino Contemplation

Saint James seeks to impart a vital message to us. He is emphasizing that belief in God is simply not enough. It is a both/and situation. Even demons believe in God's existence and acknowledge that there is one God, yet they are not virtuous creatures, nor does this mere belief redeem them. Their belief does not lead them to submit to God's authority in obedience.

From the depths of his passion and love for Christ born from his own walk with the Creator, Saint James implores us to remember that faith without works is dead, useless, and worthless. He offers the powerful example of the patriarch Abraham, who demonstrated his faith in God by being willing to sacrifice his own son (a profound and symbolic story found in Genesis 22). This harrowing tale finds redemption when his son is spared, replaced by a sacrificial ram. This moment foreshadows Christ as the Lamb of God, taking our place on the cross. Jesus Christ demonstrated His love through His death, bringing redemption to those who believe.

Abraham had faith in God, and his faith compelled him to

perform an act of obedience. This act was then credited to him as faith and redemption from his old way of life. His union of faith and works achieved the ultimate purpose: salvation from the path of darkness and destruction.

Faith is more than mere belief; it is living differently because of our belief in God, transforming our lives and actions in response to His love.

Practical Application

Belief in Jesus is proved by obedience and faith.

St. James Writes

James 2: 19 *You believe that there is one God; you are right. But the demons also believe that and tremble.* **20** *Do you even want to know, O foolish man, that faith without works is useless?* **21** *Was not Abraham our patriarch justified by works when he offered up Isaac his son upon the altar?* **22** *You see that faith worked with his actions, and by works his faith achieved its purpose.*

Prayer for the Peregrino

Dear Lord, thank you for giving me faith to trust in you. I humbly ask You to help me to demonstrate my faith in You by doing works of kindness and love for others. Thank you for taking my place as the sacrificial Lamb. I trust in You alone.

In Christ's Name, Amen.

FIFTEENTH DAY

"Life is about accepting the challenges
along the way, choosing to keep moving
forward, and savoring the journey

- Roy T. Bennett, *The Light in the Heart*

The Path from Astorga to Rabanal del Camino

The ascent into the mountains is a gentle one, the pilgrims making their way up with ease. The surroundings still boast the mighty oak and fragrant pine trees, but as the air grows cooler and thinner, the small and nameless stone villages they pass through appear abandoned, as if recently ghosted. Yet, in some of these hamlets, the locals of the *Maragatos* clan still reside. These mysterious people have survived through centuries of wars and conquests, their suspiciousness of outsiders ingrained from the ever-present threat of annihilation.

La Maragatería, the home of this unique group, is a place where tradition is being slowly lost, although efforts to preserve their way of life can be found in Astorga. The fair-skinned Maragatos, numbering only a few thousand, are believed to have been former Goths who converted to Islam, reconverted to Christianity, or perhaps remained as Mozarabs under the Moors. Their exact origins remain obscured in the past, but it is likely that their people include a mix of wartime refugees who joined the old mountain settlements centuries ago.

Their dress is quite expressive and distinct, and in Astorga, the Maragatos of today seek to preserve and celebrate their traditions. They are dressed just as beautifully as the Banjara people of South India with their gaudy jewelry and lavish head dresses. The men of the Maragatos can be easily identified with their mostly black attire contrasted with brightly colored finery, including a prominent red garter and big black felt-type hats called a slouch hat. The women wear colorful shawls draped over their shoulders, hanging down to just about the rim of their black skirts, along with a head covering that is reminiscent of the old Mozarabic fashion of unconverted Christians living under Muslim rule.

The telltale architecture of their houses is that of single-story mason-stoned buildings topped with slate or, more uncommonly, thatch. This style of house, called *teitada*, is unique in its shorter construction and unique rooftops. Each home has small windows that help preserve any warmth from their fireplace during the brutal winters. The entrance is an oversized parking entrance reminiscent of the time of horse-drawn carriages, except that the Maragatos were known as muleteers for their mules rather than horses.

As pilgrims make their way towards Rabanal del Camino or Foncebadón, a few kilometers further up the road, the topography of the land changes drastically from that of the lowlands of the Central Plateau they have left behind. Having passed through El Ganso, where pilgrims can easily spot the old Maragato houses that sit just off the path, the landscape transforms into one dominated by wild thyme and pale purple heather. While the oak trees are still present, their forests begin to thin due to the high winds and harsh weather conditions of the mountain pass. A scrubby and unpleasant brush starts to grow in patches, and the rich soil of the Castilian Meseta has eroded away completely, leaving the mountain ground rocky with quartz - a sign of the presence of gold somewhere nearby. And indeed, the old mines can be found by those willing to make a detour.

The mountains loom before the pilgrims, their rounded peaks protruding heavenward. As the pilgrims continue their ascent, they find that the rugged mountains themselves offer a lesson in resilience and determination. Each one provokes a challenge to conquer the unimaginable. The Maragatos, too, embody this spirit of perseverance, their traditions serving as a testament to their enduring culture. The shifting landscapes of the mountains serve as a reminder that life is ever-changing, and that growth comes from learning to adapt to these transformations. With each weary step, the pilgrims find their resolve strengthened, their spirits renewed, and their hearts open to the possibilities that lay ahead.

Camino Contemplation

Like the rugged landscape of the mountains, the path is challenging. The initial excitement of walking the Way of Saint

James has faded, leaving us with the raw essence of the journey. The purposes of pilgrimage are as diverse as the people who traverse the path, but one thing unites each traveler: faith.

Sometimes it is faith in oneself, sometimes faith in a higher power, or sometimes even when faith seems lost, and all that remains is the next step ahead.

Saint James experienced similar moments when his faith was shaken, particularly when Christ was betrayed by a close friend and handed over to the authorities who would persecute Him, as foretold by the ancient Jewish prophets. Yet, Saint James persevered. He allowed his shaken faith to strip away falsehoods, leaving behind a solid foundation built on Christ the Cornerstone.

Saint James continued his journey and penned a message for future generations. He solidified these thoughts on faith by further examining Abraham and providing another example—a prostitute whose wicked lifestyle was transformed by her virtuous deeds and faith in God. Mercy reached down, granting redemption to her and her household. She was healed.

The journey will undoubtedly be rough. At times, life may feel like a sinking swamp of vice, a harsh scrubland tearing at our fragile bodies. However, we can find solace in knowing that Saint James, who knew Christ intimately, reassures us that any and all evil is conquered by the power of the living Christ. Love covers a multitude of sins, mercy triumphs over judgment, and we are capable of doing good works; all we need is a little faith.

Practical Application

Faith remains alive by doing good deeds. Without them, faith is as good as dead.

St. James Writes

James 2: 23 *The scripture was fulfilled which says, "Abraham believed God, and it was credited to him as righteousness." So Abraham was called a friend of God.* **24** *You see that by works a man is justified, and not only by faith.* **25** *In like manner also was not Rahab the prostitute justified by works, when she welcomed the messengers and sent them away by another road?* **26** *For as the body apart from the spirit is dead, likewise faith apart from works is dead.*

Prayer for the Peregrino

Dear Lord, thank you for believing in me. I humbly ask You to give me deeper faith in You, that I, like Abraham, may be called Your friend. I trust You to help me say no to vice, but to walk in Your truth and the path of life.

In Christ's Name, Amen.

SIXTEENTH DAY

"And above all, watch with glittering eyes the whole world around you because the greatest secrets are always hidden in the most unlikely places."

- Roald Dahl, British novelist

The Mountains of Maragatería

In the rugged mountains, where every resource must be utilized, the locals waste nothing. Chorizo, a staple food originating in the Iberian Peninsula, is made from pork that has been preserved or cured using various techniques. The meat is chopped and mixed with spices like paprika and garlic before being formed into tubes and dried. Longer and thinner chorizos are often sweeter than their stubbier and thicker counterparts, and they are used to flavor dishes or served on tapas with cheese, bread, and wine.

Maragato stew is the most renowned dish of Maragaterian cuisine and is served as a hearty three-course meal. The first course consists of a plate of salty hot meats and sausages, followed by a plate of savory vegetables. The meal concludes with a robust pasta soup and freshly baked bread, if available.

To prepare the stew, a variety of sausages and meats such as pork snout, ear, and trotter, are combined with chicken, beef, and occasionally goat meat, if available. They are then boiled with chickpeas until tender. In a separate dish, tubers like potatoes and carrots are boiled along with chopped cabbage. The tender cabbage is then collected, strained, and fried in olive oil with fresh chopped garlic. It is seasoned with smoked paprika and added back to the potatoes and carrots. The flavorful chickpeas are then added on top of the vegetables, followed by pasta cooked in the broth from the meats and chickpeas until ready to serve. It is no surprise that this dish is a favorite among mountain dwellers.

Five hundred years ago, on his return to Spain, Columbus brought back an elongated pepper with a deep red color that was native to the Americas. This pepper became popular as a seasoning and preservative and was cultivated in the central-western part of Spain, about 500 miles south of La Maragatería, where it continues to be produced en masse to this day. Extremadura, a place that borders Portugal, is where this popular spice is cultivated. In Spanish, it is called *pimentón*, while in English, it is known as *paprika*. Paprika is made from these elongated red peppers, which are distant relatives of today's bell peppers. They are dried and smoked with oak wood, and sometimes even tobacco in the wetter regions.

While most of the smoked paprika grown in Spain today is not as spicy as it used to be before it adapted to the soils of Spain, *pimentón picante* is a spicy version that can be found. *Pimentón agridulce* is the not-as-spicy version, while the regular "sweet" version is labeled *pimentón dulce*.

Spanish paprika, which lends its color to red chorizo and its deep flavor to various dishes like tapas, paella, and Maragato stew, became a pillar in Spanish cuisine and spread throughout Europe and the territories under the former Ottoman Empire. Although Hungarian peppers come from Iberian ones, Spanish paprika is different from the popular Hungarian paprika which has a sweeter flavor due to the climate in that region. *Paprika*, the Hungarian word for the spice, is used today.

Camino Contemplation

When it comes to drawing closer to God, embracing the power of silence is a potent tool. Jesus Christ Himself practiced this art, often retreating to the mountains and wilderness to pray and meditate. But when Jesus spoke, interesting things happened. Through His example, many Christian mystics and saints have learned to connect with God on a profoundly deep level.

To be in God's presence is an incredible experience. Some connect with God better through music, others connect with God better in nature. Both are great ways to worship! Wherever we are, we must learn to practice a type of contemplative prayer in which we are actively listening to God. He speaks and will respond to us in His still, small voice. *Listening prayer* is a skill. And like any art form, we must exercise and practice to grow and develop. Prayer, in one of its forms, is simply a dialogue with God Himself. And if we learn to silence the distractions of the world, we will actually hear Him speak to us.

The Book of James reminds us of the sheer might of our words. For they can either bring life or death, depending on how they are used. Saint James warns us not to be loquacious, for it is not the quantity of our words that makes us wise, but rather the quality of them. He cautions us against seeking a position of teaching for the sake of having power over people.

As we traverse through this journey of life, let us always keep in mind the words we speak. May we strive to use our words to bring life and love to those around us. May we also embrace the power of silence as a means of deepening our bond with God. Remember that we are all teachers in one way or another, and we will be judged more harshly by the words we use. So, let us choose our words with wisdom, and let us use them to uplift and encourage those around us.

Practical Application

Be careful of what you say and how you say it.

St. James Writes

James 3: 1 *Not many of you should become teachers, my brothers, knowing that we will receive greater judgment.* **2** *For we all stumble in many ways. If anyone does not stumble in his words, he is a perfect man, able to control his whole body also.* **3** *Now if we put the horses' bits into their mouths they obey us, and we can turn their whole bodies.* **4** *Notice also that ships, although they are so large and are driven by strong winds, are steered by a very small rudder wherever the pilot desires to turn.* **5** *Likewise the tongue is a small body part, yet boasts great things.*

Prayer for the Peregrino

Dear Lord, thank you for teaching me that silence is okay. I humbly ask You to help me speak only that which is pleasing in Your sight, that my words will be words of life and truth. May my words be few, but let them be seasoned with Your virtue and demonstrated with good deeds.

In Christ's Name, Amen.

SEVENTEENTH DAY

"If you want to walk fast, walk alone. If you want to walk far, walk together."

- African Proverb

The Path from Rabanal to Foncebadón

The morning mist hung like a veil of mystery, obscuring the breathtaking panoramic views of the mountains. Instead of beautiful scenery, the Pilgrim was met with a thick, indistinct fog and a sunless sky that unleashed cold rain in a curious, intermittent manner. Like a mischievous child playing with a hose, the rain soaked everything for a few seconds before abruptly stopping.

Walking through the early morning cold, the Pilgrim couldn't ignore the blisters on his feet, dressed but still present. Not-quite-fully-dry socks added to the discomfort. Fingers and nose tips were in desperate need of warmth, but a friend lent an extra pair of gloves that, despite the fingertips being cut off for greater dexterity, provided a much-needed layer of protection.

The path grew steeper and slipperier as the pilgrims ascended. Finally, they stumbled upon a stony café that looked as if a schoolboy had built a fort during summertime. The shelter was filled with odd ends and bits of material to keep out the elements, but the cold mountain wind still seeped in through wide-open spaces. The pilgrims huddled around an open fire that heated a blackened kettle of hot water, passing hot cups of tea and coffee around and basking in the warmth. Although the

Pilgrim wished to stay in this rugged little *refugio* longer, the cup was quickly emptied, and the journey continued.

Earlier that morning, a large group of pilgrims had departed from Rabanal, where the Knights Templar had maintained a special outpost to protect local mining efforts and pilgrims en route to Ponferrada, over 20 miles away. Continuing along the extended ridge line of Monte Irago, the path led through the 2000-year-old hamlet of Foncebadón, where pilgrims could find the last traces of the Maragatos and their rugged stone walls before moving into the region of El Bierzo.

Ahead, the infamous Cruz de Ferro awaited.

As the world stumbled out of the so-called Dark Ages, a period of European history when much of the populace was without scientific or mature spiritual knowledge, the power of ideas began to spread like wildfire. Just 25 years after Columbus set sail from Spain, the famed iconoclast and reformer Martin Luther nailed a collection of counter-ideas that exposed the unjust spiritual authority of the day. As an Augustinian friar who had been ordained into the priesthood, Luther was well acquainted with learning and teaching others. He realized that reading the Bible himself brought a spiritual enlightenment that was being covered up by the so-called keepers of truth. However, instead of opening the door wide for all to enter, the layman was reduced to working and paying money to earn God's favor and grace.

Martin Luther taught that all believers in Christ are a part of the priesthood. This challenged the authority of the Catholic church and provided a path for the common man to connect with God directly. Furthermore, he argued that we don't need another mediator between us and God because only Jesus Christ can be the intermediary, a feat that was accomplished by Christ's death on the Cross. He also taught people how to get to God, and even translated the holy Scriptures into the common language of ordinary people. His ideas revolutionized the way people practiced their spirituality.

Suddenly, God was no longer perceived as a distant God, but He was *Emmanuel*: right here with us! Luther was excommunicated for these dissenting ideas. No longer were people required to work or pay for salvation, but rather, through faith in Jesus Christ, they could receive God's grace and love. Luther's teachings were radical, but they resonated with many who were seeking a deeper connection with God.

As these ideas spread, they had a profound impact on the Camino de Santiago. Why pay for something that is offered freely? Many people stopped walking the Camino to earn salvation and towns suffered with the lessening of the walking patrons. But then later, they started walking it as a pilgrimage of self-discovery and spiritual growth. The decline of towns and hamlets along the route was reversed, and places like Foncebadón began to come back to life. Entrepreneurs and investors poured resources into the local economies, and the communities that had once been forgotten were revitalized.

Thanks to the resurgence of pilgrims over the last few centuries, the Camino de Santiago continues to be a spiritual journey for people of all faiths and backgrounds. It is a reminder that we all have the power to connect with God directly and that salvation is not something that can be bought or earned.

Camino Contemplation

The Camino offers us a chance to discover ourselves and build new relationships with fellow pilgrims. With each step we take, we have the opportunity to grow in faith and strengthen our connection with God. As we walk, we learn how to become more Christlike. And by talking with strangers, we form meaningful connections with those we meet along the way.

Saint James continues to remind us of the consequences of what we say. He notes that our tongues are unruly, like wild animals that can't be tamed. Only by walking with Christ can we find the help we need to continually use our words in a way that is honorable.

As you walk in solitude and reflection, take this opportunity to connect with Christ and seek His guidance. Let Him lead your words and use them to bring encouragement and positivity to those around you. Remember that you are not alone on this journey. Christ walks beside you every step of the way.

Practical Application

What you say is powerful. Use this power wisely.

St. James Writes

James 3: 6 *The tongue is also a fire, a world of sinfulness. The tongue is set among our body parts, staining the whole body and setting on fire the course of life. But it is itself set on fire by hell.* **7** *For every kind of wild animal, bird, reptile, and sea creature is being tamed and has been tamed by mankind.* **8** *But no human being can tame the tongue. It is a restless evil, full of deadly poison.* **9** *With it we praise the Lord and Father, and with it we curse men, who have been made in the likeness of God.*

Prayer for the Peregrino

Dear Lord, thank you for the strength to speak well of ourselves and others as we speak to others along the way. And as the Psalmist also prayed, may the words of my mouth and the meditations of my heart be acceptable in Your sight, Jehovah God, my Rock and my Redeemer.

In Christ's Name, Amen.

EIGHTEENTH DAY

"In every walk with nature, one receives far more than he seeks."

- John Muir, Scottish-born US naturalist

The Path from Foncebadón to the Cruz de Ferro

Stopping at the last place in Foncebadón before the final ascent, the Pilgrim purchased a muesli granola bar, handmade in the old stone building. The softness of the oats and dried fruits provides sweet calories, the perfect fuel for the mountains.

The rocky landscape is both rugged and beautiful, much like the journey itself. Forests of juniper pine flanked by oak trees provide relief from the receding inclement weather.

In a time when people were largely illiterate, the literate were relied upon to read Holy Scripture aloud to the masses. The Roman Catholic Church had declared that only the theologically educated could read and explain the mysteries of God, and for good reason; this helped to ensure that heretical teachings were not propagated. Furthermore, public readings of the Bible were largely in Latin, a language not understood by the common Spanish speaker. Though fragments and portions of the Bible had been meticulously copied and passed around, the entire Holy Bible, including the writings of Saint James, were largely kept within the small circles of educated and devoted clergy as well as wealthy patrons, leaving the common man and pilgrim unable to access Scripture.

With the Council of Tarragona of 1234 in Catalonia, Spain, all copies of the Bible in the local languages descended from Latin were ordered to be gathered and burned, making the world even darker. However, this would not last forever. In the years prior to its publication in 1569, as the *Reconquista* from the Moors began to mellow, a Spanish monk from Extremadura, the place that would soon produce the famed paprika spice, escaped the Spanish Inquisition having been marked as a heretic due to his adherence to the original Lutheranism. This man, Casiodoro de Reina, took the fragments of the Bible that had been translated into Spanish by certain communities around Spain and completed the translation as a refugee. Thanks to the development of the printing press, his work became the first printed (non-hand-copied) version in Spanish, revolutionizing the Spanish speakers of the Iberian Peninsula and beyond.

While there is always the possibility of heretics mistranslating and misinterpreting what God said through His inspired prophets, it is not a reason to restrict that which is good. Even though individuals have the free will to turn something good into evil, it doesn't mean that the good should be limited or restrained. Test everything and hold on to that which is good.

While the extent to which the written Word of God was forbidden by Roman Catholic Popes and Bishops is disputed, it remains a fact that owning or reading a Bible in one's vernacular was discouraged by many Councils and leaders throughout the ages. However, today, Catholics are encouraged to connect with the Bible, and the Path of Saint James has become less a path to salvation and more a journey of spiritual enrichment.

As the journey towards Santiago continues, the land, like following the way of Christ, is no less harsh. The crops are fewer in the mountains and the towns are smaller, their inhabitants seemingly absent, having presumably moved their sheep and cows to greener pastures.

Wedges of white quartz and sandstone continue to crunch underfoot, threatening the already tired ankles and knees. The Pilgrim is grateful for the wooden staff, which steadies his gait and holds his fatigued body erect, longing to hunch over and lie down in relief. There is a water fountain just before reaching the Cruz de Ferro, providing safe and refreshing water to drink, much like the Living Water that flows from Christ.

Camino Contemplation

Saint James was full of love for those to whom he writes. His heart was to release a blessing upon the readers of his message, which he learned from Christ. He desires purity of heart from those who say they are disciples of Christ. While he has observed some disconnect amongst those who claim allegiance to Christ, he gently exhorts us toward purity of heart and mind. Like a wise old sage, his words guide us along the straight and narrow with a simple thought.

Saint James' message to us is clear - what comes from our lives should be good, not evil. We should speak blessing, not curses. The fruit from our lives should be the good and life-giving things of God, not something else that is foreign to life in Christ. It's like a fountain that sometimes gives safe drinking water, and then at other times pours out poisonous water. If this happened, it would be listed as a non-safe place to get water. No longer life-giving water, the fountain would be condemned as dangerous.

Just like the fountain, our words and actions should produce good fruit. And when we are planted in Christ, only goodness can be produced. God is love, and He is like a stream of water. When we abide in Him through Christ Jesus, we can only produce good things that flow out from His love within us.

However, we are still in a battle against the temptations of the thief of God's light, Lucifer, whose name means "light bearer". By mixing in some truth, he tricks people into believing a lie, and we need to be careful not to fall into his traps. Only by continually abiding in the life-flow of Christ can we complete the journey God has set before us. We run our course with patience, just as we walk our Camino with patience. God is calling us up into a higher place. The invitation is there, we only need to step into it by faith.

Practical Application

Now that we have the power of Christ living within us, Only goodness and love should come from within, not darkness and evil.

St. James Writes

James 3: 10 *Out of the same mouth come blessing and cursing. My brothers, these things should not happen.* **11** *Does a spring pour out from its single opening both sweet and bitter water?* **12** *Is a fig tree, my brothers, able to make olives? Or a grapevine, figs? Neither can salty water produce sweet water.*

Prayer for the Peregrino

Dear Lord, thank you for being the source of blessings and thank you for being my source of life. Keep me, I pray, clean and let that which comes from me be pure and holy in Your sight. Let the fruit of my life be evidence of Your light within me.

In Christ's Name, Amen.

NINETEENTH DAY

"As you start to walk out on the way, the way appears."

- Rumi, Thirteenth-century Persian mystic and poet

Cruz de Ferro

At last, the Pilgrim arrived at a wide-open area encompassed by a forest of juniper and heather. There, a solemn procession of pilgrims bowed their heads in humility before the Cruz de Ferro. The small iron cross mounted atop a wooden pole was positioned at the peak of an old pile of stones assembled by the ancient pagans. Although rather plain and quite ordinary, it is humble. Without a guide, one could easily walk past without recognizing the special significance of the heap of rubble.

The pile was likely begun by the pagan Celts of the pre-Roman era who had marked their mountain pass with an unnatural pile of rocks, as was their custom. Centuries later, the Romans dedicated the pile as a monument to honor a celestial deity.

Finally, although a bit speculative, the poetic hermit Gaucelmo mounted the Iron Cross at the apex of the pile in the twelfth century, turning what was profane into something wholly sacred. Around the planet, a lot began to develop during the twelfth century. There was the building of the Hindu Temples at Angkor in Cambodia which would gradually became a Buddhist holy ground. The man who would become Genghis Khan was born in the land we call Mongolia. And the Knights Templar were founded to protect pilgrims to the Holy Land.

Decades later, the continuation of the Christian fight against the Arabs to gain Jerusalem back raged onward. Meanwhile, Muslims continued to expand their reach and stretch into the Indian subcontinent in South Asia while simultaneously being booted out of Iberia during Spain's *Reconquista*. As the Iberian Peninsula reeled from the effects of conflict, the little cross was mounted as a symbolic gesture that no matter what happens, Christ is still worth following and will show you the way forward.

Since the topping of the plain iron cross, pilgrims from around the world bring a stone from their country, or if necessary, procure a pebble somewhere in the plains of the Castilian Meseta. At the foot of the cross, they lay their burdens down along with that stone as a permanent reminder that God indeed hears their prayers and grants forgiveness and grace along the way. Some pilgrims leave pictures of loved ones, while others write notes or poems or letters and leave them there. The Pilgrim glances at a few, not wanting to intrude but curious as to who has gone before. Still, others have left mementos. There's a bandana, a pair of old sandals, a few rusting pins and old shells, a string of Tibetan prayer flags...

The Pilgrim joined the countless pilgrims who, over the last thousand years, stopped here in silent prayer and solitude of self with the Creator.

"Lord, hear my prayer too..."

The Pilgrim cannot remember whether he placed the blue stone or the orange one at the foot of the cross. All that was important was that this unlovely pile of rubble was holy ground. But it is not the time to remove one's shoes.

In some ways, it is just a pile of rubble, a pile of those things from this earth-life that we wish never happened, things we want to forget, things that we hope Christ can heal within our timid hearts. But that is the thing. God is really good at making something beautiful from the ashes and rubble. God makes peace with us. We are to make peace with ourselves and others.

Moving forward, the landscape makes a downward incline, and the thinning clusters of chestnut trees are beginning to end, practically eliminated altogether. The forest is replaced by heather, in addition to dense thickets of scrub oak.

The highest elevation on the Camino is located here, just a few spaces shy of 5,000 feet. However, passing this place doesn't mark the end of uphill climbs. There will be many more to come. For now, the steep descent on rocky terrain is proving to be a challenge for everyone's knees.

As the Pilgrim walks downward, he notices a distant plain and a small city in the distance, still hours away. The view is nothing short of spectacular, yet at the same time, it feels daunting. The clouds are beginning to clear, revealing the city of Ponferrada below, drawing closer with every step.

Amidst this breathtaking scenery, the aromatic *Rockrose* is in full bloom. Its narrow and elongated evergreen leaves are adorned with small flowers consisting of white petals clinging to a yellow center disk. The Pilgrim takes in the abundant presence of these shrubs which lend a delightful fragrance to the mountain air. The simple pleasure of taking a deep breath is a soothing balm for the Pilgrim's soul.

Camino Contemplation

Saint James fearlessly speaks the truth in love, reminding us of the distinction between true and counterfeit wisdom. The latter is evil and demonic, permeated with darkness, bitterness, and deceit. In contrast, Christ's genuine wisdom is like a fertile tree that bears the fruit of peace and love. It is crucial to distinguish between the two.

There is a connection between wisdom and righteousness and

peace. They are all intertwined together. Jesus preached in the Sermon on the Mount, 'Blessed are the peacemakers, for they will be called the children of God.'

As we journey along the Camino, let us be mindful of our thoughts and actions, ensuring that they align with Christ's wisdom. Let us strive to be peacemakers and seek God's guidance through prayer and reflection. Although we may encounter obstacles, let us boldly ask God for wisdom and the Holy Spirit's help to overcome them and continue along our path.

Practical Application

Wisdom is a gift from God. Seek peace and pursue it.

St. James Writes

James 3: 13 *Who is wise and understanding among you? Let that person show a good life by his works in the humility of wisdom.* **14** *But if you have bitter jealousy and ambition in your heart, do not boast and lie against the truth.* **15** *This is not the wisdom that comes down from above. Instead, it is earthly, unspiritual, demonic.* **16** *For where there is jealousy and ambition, there is confusion and every evil practice.* **17** *But the wisdom from above is first pure, then peaceloving, gentle, reasonable, full of mercy and good fruits, impartial and sincere.* **18** *But the fruit of righteousness is sown in peace among those who make peace.*

Prayer for the Peregrino

Dear Lord, thank you for being the source of peace. I humbly ask that You guide me along Your path today and help me to be a peacemaker.

In Christ's Name, Amen.

TWENTIETH DAY

"Only one who wanders finds new paths."

- Norwegian Proverb

Ponferrada

Finally, the Pilgrim descended the mountain and reached the city of Ponferrada at the foot of the range. With relief, he found his fellow pilgrims waiting at a café on the other side of the Meruelo River. There they pointed out a little waterway where a shallow stream had been diverted from the main river. Removing his socks and shoes, the Pilgrim submerged both his weary feet into the icy flow. It took a full minute to complete this task because the water was so cold. Finally, after one or two more dunks that rejuvenated his feet, he was ready to go to the hostel and rest.

However, the little neighborhood was only the outskirts of Ponferrada, and the Pilgrim's final resting place for the night was still another hour away. With each step, his feet felt like heavy lead, and he grumbled once again.

"Why am I even doing this?"

Determined to complete the day's hike, the Pilgrim continued through the narrow streets and side alleys of the little town of Molinaseca. Suddenly, he was stopped by a local shop owner. The Spaniard, with his jet-black hair, greeted him with a warm "¡Buen Camino, peregrino!" and asked about his journey.

The Pilgrim told him that he was heading to Ponferrada. The

man explained that this little shop belonged to him and invited the Pilgrim inside. Not in a pleasant mood, the Pilgrim declined, wanting to get to the hostel. But the shop owner pleaded with him, insisting that he didn't have to buy anything. The Pilgrim finally stepped inside and looked around, admiring the various colorful trinkets and wooden souvenirs, key rings, and local wines.

Although he was already loaded with a backpack and his last dollars had gone to new shoes, the shop owner excitedly displayed some of his handmade jewelry and necklaces in hopes he might buy one. The shop owner then showed the Pilgrim a woven bracelet with a little Christ-on-the-Cross pewter pendant dangling from the strap. The Pilgrim examined the piece, admired its beauty, and passed it back. But the shopkeeper declined. Instead, he grabbed the Pilgrim's hand and, sliding the bracelet over the Pilgrim's wrist, declared that it was a gift. "Here," he said, "it is a gift from me. You don't have to pay. Thank you for coming into my store!" The shop owner smiled, but sad eyes betrayed a lonely soul.

Feeling humiliated by the shop owner's generosity, the Pilgrim blushed with gratitude and thanked him kindly. The Pilgrim was reminded that on this journey, it wasn't just about discovering new places, but also about the kindness of strangers and the existential need for human connection.

Reflecting on this encounter, the Pilgrim felt grateful for the unexpected gift, but also for the reminder that kindness and generosity could come from unexpected places.

He remembered the story of the disciples falling asleep in the garden and understood the temptation to become complacent and indifferent. But he also realized that there was a greater purpose to his journey on the Camino, one that involved more than just his own personal growth and development. Perhaps he was there to make a difference in someone else's life, to be a source of light and encouragement in a world that was often cold and indifferent.

Passing by cherry trees and apple trees beginning to droop with some variety of immature Pippin apples, the Pilgrim eventually made his way to the hostel and stumbled through the door. That morning had started high in the mountains. Tonight he was in the Central Valley.

"I think tomorrow will be a good day to rest," he mumbled as his weary eyelids closed.

Camino Contemplation

As we travel along the Camino, Saint James encourages us to contemplate a crucial question: Where does evil come from? In his own spiritual journey, James witnessed Jesus' actions and noted that His life of virtue flowed naturally from His surrender to the Father in Heaven. Jesus did not have to struggle to be good because His submission to God allowed the Holy Spirit to flow through Him. He demonstrated that true virtue comes supernaturally.

The things that cause death in this world are not of God, but rather from the enemy who seeks to kill, steal, and destroy. Lucifer, the father of lies, tempts us with thoughts that rob us of peace, joy, and life. God loves us unconditionally and desires to have a pure and selfless love relationship with us, much like a groom loves his bride. When we turn away from loving God and give in to the ways of darkness, He fights for us with a jealous love.

Let us take up the fight for what is good and virtuous. Let us love God and reject the ways of darkness. As we continue on our spiritual journey, let us walk in peace and surrender our hearts daily to His love.

Practical Application

Faith and surrender to God are essential to living a full life. Selfish ambition is a great way to cause problems.

St. James Writes

James 4: 1 *Where do quarrels and where do disputes among you come from? Do they not come from your desires that fight among your members?* **2** *You desire, and you do not have. You kill and covet, and you are not able to obtain. You fight and quarrel. You do not possess because you do not ask.* **3** *You ask and do not receive because you ask badly, in order that you may use it for your desires.* **4** *You adulteresses! Do you not know that friendship with the world is hostility against God? So whoever wants to be a friend of the world makes himself an enemy of God.* **5** *Or do you think that the scripture says in vain, "The Spirit he caused to live in us is deeply jealous"?*

Prayer for the Peregrino

Dear Lord, thank you for showing the world Your love. Please forgive me for any evil I've committed against You. I humbly ask that You fill me with Your life today and help me to walk in Your truth.

In Christ's Name, Amen.

TWENTY-FIRST DAY

"The function of prayer is not to influence God, but rather to change the nature of the one who prays."

- Søren Kierkegaard, Nineteenth-century Danish philosopher and theologian

The Path from Ponferrada to Villafranca

Having been rebuilt after several successive invasions and destructions, the city of Ponferrada has a special bridge built over the Sil River reinforced with iron, giving it the name *Ponferrada*, a blend of words meaning "Iron Bridge". This is the capital city of the autonomous region of Castile and León.

On the banks of the Sil River lies a sprawling and magnificent fortress that once belonged to the Knights Templar. The fort, originally in ruins for many years from multiple invasions, was given to the Templars in hopes they could restore and maintain it. From their inception of nine knights protecting pilgrims in Jerusalem's Temple Mount (from whence they gleaned their name), they continued this tradition of protecting pilgrims around Europe and along the Camino de Santiago. But their sovereignty would last only 200 years before jealous discreditors absolved their rites, leading to the dismantling of their order in 1312, and ultimately the redistribution of their assets, or so the story goes.

Now, the enormous *Castillo de los Templarios* in Ponferrada stands as a monument to their work. It is equipped with the Templar Library of rare books from the Middle Ages. The castle has been conquered and reconquered time and again. Portions have been annexed, and much of the fortress has been under reconstruction for many years, like pilgrims on a journey. We as pilgrims are moved to remember the Latin motto inscribed in the entrance of the castle's central tower that, translated, says, "If the Lord does not protect the city, those who protect it guard it in vain."

Leaving the city, the Pilgrim paused to capture a photograph in front of the great castle with its moat and drawbridge. He regretted not having the time to explore its historical rooms and ancient passageways. Oh, to read the ancient books that have, without a doubt, influenced the path that brought us to the modern world. What secrets lie behind those impenetrable walls?

The path today began relatively flat, a relief from the mountain pass of recent days. The Pilgrim continued through the isolated upper basin of El Bierzo province in León. It was a two-day walk through the isolated valley before climbing up into the mountains again. The shape of the undulating land was a terrestrial version of the Atlantic Ocean, rolling motionless to and fro.

The mineral-rich countryside was blanketed with once completely hand-harvested vineyards. Modern machinery and agricultural practices now handle the majority of the harvesting mechanically. The rows of grapevines were perfectly distanced from one another and, from a distance, drew attention to a world of mesmerizing symmetry.

Chestnut trees were peppered throughout. Regional staples included obscure cuts of pork meat like tail and rib stuffed into pig intestine, flavored with paprika and garlic, and finally smoked. Called *Botillo del Bierzo*, this sausage could be seen hanging from shops and windows as pilgrims passed by. The aroma of fire-roasted red peppers called *Pimiento Asado del Bierzo* wafted throughout the numerous charming and quiet towns. Chestnuts were available on tables for donations, and fresh-squeezed orange juice was advertised, all making the stomach grumble.

Camino Contemplation

Saint James reminds us of the holiness of God. God is absolute purity, and anything in His presence is transformed into its purest form. By surrendering to Him, we too become holy. This is a great grace-gift from God, purchased with a hefty price - Christ's death on the cross. It's not a cheap gift, but it is freely available to all who accept it.

God has given us free will, the ability to choose what we want. If we want to experience joy, peace, and a good life, God instructs us to follow His ways. The results of following Christ are life-giving fruits that bring prosperity, hope, and a flourishing future. The Holy Scriptures offer us guidance and wisdom to live in alignment with God's will.

Saint James makes it clear that there is no middle ground - we are either submitting to God or resisting His ways. If we resist God, then we are submitting our lives to the guidance of Lucifer, the evil enemy of God. This leads to resistance from God in our lives. God is trying to protect us from the path of a lifelong resistance to Himself, which ultimately leads to death and destruction.

But we have been given the grace-gift of strength to resist the devil. We resist by intentionally drawing close to God in the best way we know how, and God will guide us. Saint James teaches us that humility is the key to this. It is an act of cleansing and purification, where our humiliation and grief for committing evil bring us closer to God.

God is always with us, but when we intentionally draw near to Him, He becomes our bodyguard, protecting us like a good parent over their vulnerable children. Resisting God is a grave matter that James warns us not to take lightly. But we receive grace and forgiveness from God, who helps us along the way.

Remember, God wants the best for us, and His ways lead to life. Let us choose to follow Him and resist the devil, drawing near to God in humility and surrender. May we be strengthened by His grace-gifts and protected by His love, as we walk our spiritual journey with confidence and faith.

Practical Application

God is always there to help us if we are willing to humble ourselves and submit to His Kingship.

St. James Writes

James 4: 6 *But God gives more grace, so the scripture says, "God opposes the proud, but gives grace to the humble." **7** So submit to God. But resist the devil, and he will flee from you. **8** Come close to God, and he will come close to you. Cleanse your hands, you sinners, and purify your hearts, you double-minded. **9** Grieve and mourn and cry! Let your laughter turn into sadness and your joy into gloom. **10** Humble yourselves before the Lord, and he will lift you up.*

Prayer for the Peregrino

Dear Lord, thank you for extending your grace toward me. I humbly ask that You help me to be humble before You. Help me to resist anything that would come in between our relationship together. Thank you for being good. I trust You.

In Christ's Name, Amen.

TWENTY-SECOND DAY

"Walk with the wise, and you will become wise."

- Jewish Proverb

The Path from Villafranca del Bierzo to O Cebreiro

Early the next day, the Pilgrim set out once again. The hostel from the night before had a large round window in the upper room with many bunk beds for pilgrims. Not until he was far down the road would the Pilgrim realize that he had left his poncho at the hostel. Saddened by the loss, he hoped it wouldn't rain for the rest of his time on the Camino. But that was not likely. While it was a luxurious and useful tool, it was another reminder to let go of the things in life that truly don't matter in the long run. It was a gift from his father and served its purpose for a time, but there are more important things in life to worry about than getting a little rained on.

A few days before in Astorga, the Pilgrim and his group had gathered to discuss the writings of Saint James. Among them was Fabio, an Italian by birth who was making the pilgrimage to decide if he wanted to take his final vows as a Franciscan friar or to discern if God would have him choose another path.

"Fabio, this is a big decision! Monks are celibate. Have you, you know, been with any women before?" someone asked him with a good-natured and mischievous smirk.

Fabio replied sheepishly, "Sir, I have not always been a friar..."

As the group of pilgrims made their way toward Galicia, Fabio joined them. Many locals are now speaking Galician, a Romance language similar to Portuguese. There is another ascent towards more high mountain ridges, the continuation of the Cantabrian Mountains. The fertile valley in El Bierzo would have been an ideal place to retire. One could live well on sheep, wine, and apples.

Villafranca, the last major town of Castile and León, marks the beginning of the last and final autonomous region of Galicia. The convergence of the Burbia and Valcarce rivers made it an ideal location for settlement for French pilgrims who gave the village its name some time back. Villafranca is a well-preserved old town, and its creative artists and vendors add to the town's unique atmosphere.

Pilgrims who started in France have walked through La Rioja and the beautiful vineyards of the Ebro Valley, Navarre, with its Gothic and Basque designs, and through Pamplona with its famous annual bull run. They have also traversed the desert of the Iberian Plateau, gone up into the mountains, and back down again. The region has been marked by Renaissance churches, endless cups of red wine, and the beginning of a journey to be left in the archives of memory.

As we leave behind the well-trodden path of Castile and León, the world is changing. Continuing on the journey, we can feel the subtle shift in the air as we approach the end of our pilgrimage. There are more picturesque villages and bridges, each with its unique charm and character. The path is bottlenecking from the other routes, gradually becoming more crowded with fellow pilgrims who are also nearing the end of their own journeys. It's a reminder to stay present and focused on the here and now, rather than worrying about what comes after.

The path is lined with deciduous horse chestnut trees, providing much-needed shade as pilgrims make the ascent. However, the actual chestnuts themselves are inedible, encased in a thorny husk.

The elevation gain increases as we trek upwards. At certain clearings, we might catch a glimpse of the ruins of the ninth-century Sarracín Castle sitting on a peak, a reminder of the rich history that surrounds us on this journey.

Each step forward is like running in a dream, with the beautiful and inspiring landscape a constant companion on the journey. Despite the physical challenges and fatigue that come with the long walk, the Pilgrim continues to push forward, knowing that the end goal of reaching Santiago de Compostela is within reach.

Camino Contemplation

The way of Christ is the way of humility, and these two paths are intimately intertwined. Saint James continues to press on us the importance of humility, especially in the context of judging others. We seek to be like Christ, our ultimate example.

Saint James tells us that there is one lawgiver and one judge. Our role as disciples of Christ is to follow humbly, not to judge others. The authority to judge belongs to God alone. When we speak against others and judge them according to the law, we inflate our own ego and pride, which is counterproductive.

As we walk our path today, let us walk in humility, speaking only words of kindness about our friends, family, and everyone else we encounter. In doing so, we will bring joy and peace to all.

Practical Application

We are all human, so treat one another with dignity and respect.

St. James Writes

James 4: 11 *Do not speak against one another, brothers. The person who speaks against a brother or judges his brother speaks against the law and judges the law. But if you judge the law, you are not a doer* of the law, but a judge. **12** Only one is the lawgiver and judge. He is the one who is able to save and to destroy. But who are you, you who judge your neighbor?

Prayer for the Peregrino

Dear Lord, thank you for being the perfect example of humility. I pray that I may walk humbly before You today. I humbly ask that You help me to love my neighbor as myself, and not to judge another.

In Christ's Name, Amen.

TWENTY-THIRD DAY

"It always seems impossible until it's done."

- Nelson Mandela, South African activist

Entering the Autonomous Region of Galicia

As the Pilgrim journeys into Galicia, the landscape transforms into a lush and verdant paradise. A solitary cow grazes contentedly in the hills, surrounded by the vibrant green pastures that stretch out. The air is thick with the scent of wildflowers, and the Pilgrim's heart swells with gratitude at the beauty of God's creation.

The stone monolith demarcating the border between Castile and León and Galicia is a reminder of the journey the Pilgrim has taken so far. It serves as a signpost of sorts, marking the way forward into the final leg of the journey. The path steepens, and the ascent becomes almost unbearable. The Pilgrim's muscles ache, and his breathing is labored. He pauses for a moment to catch his breath, and his eyes are drawn to more cows, who seem oblivious to the difficulty of the terrain.

The Galician region is known for its abundance of seafood dishes, bell peppers, pear-shaped cheeses, white kidney beans, and, of course, its red and white wines. The rivers that flow through the land are so numerous that the region is known as the "country of a thousand rivers." Despite its fertile soils and ease of access to food from the ocean, Galicia has avoided the growth of massive cities, maintaining a sense of simplicity and connection to the land.

As the Pilgrim climbs higher into the mountains, his thoughts turn inward. He wonders about the people who call these hills home. Are they happy, living in harmony with the natural world that surrounds them? Do they understand the beauty and majesty of the land they call home?

The Pilgrim's tall wooden walking staff has become a trusted companion, worn and frayed from the many miles it has traveled. Its blunt end rests firmly on the ground, providing support and stability as the Pilgrim climbs. The blisters on his hands have healed, and his shoes, though showing signs of wear, have held up admirably.

With each step, the Pilgrim draws closer to his goal. Though the path ahead may be steep and treacherous, he knows that God is with him, providing strength and guidance along the way. He takes a deep breath, relishing the cool mountain air, and continues on his journey with renewed determination and purpose.

The little cafés and eateries begin to offer the Galician Torta de Santiago. This special sweet sponge cake has a powdered sugar imprint of the Cross of Saint James on the top, and it is a century-old tradition in which the zesty pastry is made with almonds and brandy. While simple in flavor, it is hearty for pilgrims who can appreciate a bite or two of this cake as they walk the path. One can imagine it to be a staple during the cold winter months.

Later that night, in O Cebreiro, the Pilgrim will taste this spongy Torta de Santiago for the first time. But before that, the path takes the Pilgrim through the Valley of Valcarce with its obsolete ruins of Sarracín Castle and the numerous vegetable gardens growing in strength along the river. From here, the journey continues through Ruitelán, offering an impressive view of the A-6 road bridging far above the path. From there, pilgrims will continue climbing the steep and demanding track through the dark woods of oak and chestnut in the small mountain enclave of Laguna de Castilla.

Pilgrims might begin to notice grain stores called *horreos*. These traditional granaries are found everywhere in this region and look like small houses with thatched or stone rooftops. Slits in the sides allow the grain to dry out and breathe. Many are elevated upon what looks like stone mushrooms atop which the little granary sits. Elevation helps keep the grain dry and preserved, as well as keeping rodents and other pests from accessing the stores of grain.

Camino Contemplation

Saint James had a profound perspective on life. He wanted to instill in us a new outlook on our time and intentions. We know that plans in life can change, but when they do, we should submit ourselves to God, knowing that His perspective is much better than our own. In the book of Jeremiah, God tells us that He has plans for us, plans for peace and not for disaster, to give us a future and a hope. When we call out to God and pray, He listens to us, and when we seek Him with all our hearts, we will find Him.

But if we're honest, it's not always easy to trust that God knows best, especially when our plans change unexpectedly. However, when we are submitted to Christ, we gain His desires within us, and we can trust that He will guide us in the right direction. We can still make plans, but our perspective should be that God knows best and will direct us along the way. We should trust Him to do so. As we journey together on the Camino, let us remember that we walk with Christ and Saint James, who went before us. Just as the path on the Camino may change, so too may our plans in life. Our plans will be supernaturally directed by God for our good and His glory.

Practical Application

Make plans and trust God to direct your steps.

St. James Writes

James 4: 13 *Now listen, you who say, "Today or tomorrow we will go into this city, and spend a year there, and trade, and make a profit."* ***14*** *You who does not know what will happen tomorrow, what is your life? For you are a mist that appears for a little while and then disappears.* ***15*** *Instead, you should say, "If the Lord wishes, then we will live and do this or that."* ***16*** *But now you are boasting about your arrogant plans. All such boasting is evil.* ***17*** *So for anyone who knows to do good but does not do it, for him it is sin.*

Prayer for the Peregrino

Dear Lord, thank you for giving me a fresh perspective on life. Lord, as I make my plans in life, I ask that You guide me along the way that I should go. Thank you for helping me every step of the way. I trust

ZEBULUN MATTOS

You and Your judgment.

In Christ's Name, Amen.

TWENTY-FOURTH DAY

"Life is a long pilgrimage from fear to love."

- Paulo Coelho, Brazilian novelist

O Cebreiro

The public hostel was full, and some pilgrims had to settle for more expensive but private rooms in other smaller guesthouses. The cold mountain air enveloped the town, making the hot shower a welcomed encounter. The small isolated village saddles a ridge on the Cebreiro pass, providing an awe-inspiring view of the Sierra de Ancares to the northeast, the Courel Mountains to the southwest, and other peaks in the Galician Massif in the northwestern region of the Iberian Peninsula.

Seated at a rustic wooden table for an early supper in the local restaurant, the Pilgrim looked around the medieval room, expecting to see dwarves and hobbits. Instead, pilgrims from different parts of the world chatted away in various languages. The Pilgrim headed up to the bar, where the waiter greeted him in Galician, "Bo serán! Good evening!" The Pilgrim ordered *Pote Gallego*, a traditional soup of Galicia, made with cabbage, collard greens, or turnip greens, onions, potatoes, white beans, and various kinds of meats, with Spanish chorizo being a must. The delicious soup is slow-cooked all day long which results in tender meat with hearty flavors. As the soup is delivered, the waiter wishes the Pilgrim a pleasant meal with "Bo proveito!"

As they eat, a fellow pilgrim prepares to share a story. The sun sets behind the ridge, and a sudden draft of cold mountain air tickles the hairs on their necks. They huddle closer to their soup bowls for warmth as the story begins. According to tradition, the Holy Grail, the cup used by Jesus Christ himself at the Last Supper, was once kept in the mountains in the little stone church in this very village. One winter day, a lone priest was blessing the Eucharist in the empty building during a severe snowstorm. As he prayed, the church door opened suddenly, and one of the faithful stumbled into the little stone room with the blizzard of snow and ice just behind them. Shocked, the priest scolded the peasant for making the treacherous pilgrimage in the middle of the storm just to make mass. But as he said this, immediately, the bread and wine transfigured into human flesh and blood, bewildering the priest and the onlooking peasant. The priest was humbled, and the peasant was honored. Through this story, Christ emphasized that simple acts of faith are the greatest miracles in His Kingdom.

Although most of the original church building is gone, some parts remain in bigger museums in other cities. A new church has been built on top of where the old one once stood, serving as a symbol of faith and spiritual strength in the face of challenges.

The *palloza* houses in O Cebreiro stand as a testament to the resilience and ingenuity of the people who built them. The oval-shaped structures, with no chimneys and an aerodynamic design, were constructed to withstand the harsh conditions of the high mountains, where unforgiving winds and inclement weather could pose a threat to any dwelling. The rooftops, made of broom plants tied together, served a dual purpose - to allow smoke from warming fires inside to escape, and to provide a place to hang and smoke-cure the farm-raised meats.

The inside of the *palloza* houses was divided into two parts - one for sheltering the farm animals and the other for the family's living space. The raised platform in the living area was used for sleeping. During the winter, the smoke from the fires would heat up the snow, which would then melt off the roof, ensuring that the structure wouldn't collapse under the weight of accumulated snow.

Although these traditional homes are no longer used for living, they have been restored and repurposed. Some have been converted into restaurants where pilgrims can enjoy a meal in the unique atmosphere. Others have been transformed into small museums, offering visitors a glimpse into the life of the people who once called these *palloza* houses their homes.

Camino Contemplation

Today, Saint James' teaching may seem a bit apocalyptic, but we can use this light to shine in the darkness and guide us towards a life of virtue. We know that Saint James walked with Christ, and his teachings come from a heart of love to help us along our spiritual journey.

Let us consider his message with sober minds. The concept is simple: do not trust in earthly riches, as they will all fade away one day. This is inevitable. Our true riches are found in Christ and His way of life. In Him, we can find a treasure that will not rust, corrupt, or be stolen.

At the same time, Saint James calls our attention to the concept of generosity. If we are fortunate enough to accumulate earthly riches, but we are stingy with what we pay to our employees or with those in need, then this warning is especially given to us.

As we walk our path today, let us remember that money is a tool, not a treasure. Our true treasure is found in Christ alone. It is found in our relationship with Him and the love we share with others during our temporary journey on earth before the ultimate reality of eternal life with Christ.

May we be inspired to use our resources wisely and generously, trusting in the abundance of God's grace and blessings in our lives. Let us continue to walk with Christ and Saint James on this pilgrimage of faith, always keeping our hearts focused on the true treasures of life.

Practical Application

Focus on what is important: your relationship with God.

St. James Writes

James 5 : 1 *Come now, you who are rich, weep and wail because of the miseries coming on you.* ***2*** *Your riches have rotted, and your clothes have become moth-eaten.* ***3*** *Your gold and your silver have become tarnished and their rust will be a witness against you. It will consume your flesh like fire. You have stored up your treasure for the last days.* ***4*** *Look, the pay of the laborers is crying out—the pay that you have withheld from those who harvested your fields, and the cries of the harvesters have gone into the ears of the Lord of hosts.* ***5*** *You have lived in luxury on the earth and indulged yourselves. You have fattened your hearts for a day of slaughter.* ***6*** *You have condemned and killed the righteous person. He does not resist you.*

Prayer for the Peregrino

Dear Lord, thank you for being the greatest treasure I could ever possess. Help me to remember that money is a tool, not a treasure. Help me to be generous toward others in my time and resources. Thank you for helping me walk your path. I trust that You are good.

In Christ's Name, Amen.

TWENTY-FIFTH DAY

"An early morning walk is a blessing for the whole day."

- Henry David Thoreau, US poet

The Path from O Cebreiro to Tricastela

It was in O Cebreiro that the Pilgrim left behind his newfound friend, Fabio. There, Fabio was reunited with his brothers, who together were making this pilgrimage to decide if they too would swear their final vows as friars of the Franciscan order. Fabio would stay behind with his confraternity in O Cebreiro for some time in prayer and contemplation. The Pilgrim, blessing Fabio with a small prayer, embraced his friend in a solemn farewell. Fabio said goodbye. He was dressed in a brown robe that draped to the floor. A simple white cincture wrapped snugly around his robe and had three knots representing poverty, chastity, and obedience.

The Pilgrim knew he would likely never see Fabio again.

Early the next morning, while leaving the saddleback hamlet, the Pilgrim strummed a small guitar along the high mountain pass as the journey continued. The ridge line, flowing up and down in the sky, provided spectacular and panoramic views of the distant ranges of Os Ancares and O Courel, breaking through the early morning fog that would clear up later in the day. The small trees and shrubs grew in abundance and consisted of yellow flowered Scotch broom, blue lilies, wild absinthe, and wild garlic. The Pilgrim continued walking on through the little villages and mountain woodlands of birch trees, pine, and ash, as well as evergreen holly with its clumps of red berries.

Somewhere, a sign read "Beware of wolves." It is in these shady patches of forests that the elusive Iberian wolves call home. The guidebooks observe how the wolves have signatory marks on the muzzle and upper lips that are white in color. Additionally, roaming about are wild boar concealed in the thick underbrush. Along with other fuzzy woodland creatures, the wild boar are wary of their predator, the wolf. Still, the path is lined with natural beauty, such as hazelnut trees, blackberry shrubs, and prickly hawthorn. Then there is the odd rye field situated amongst the vineyards that grow even in this rough land.

Continuing along Mount Oribio at Alto de San Roque, there stands a stalwart bronze statue of Santiago, walking resolutely and holding his hat to his head amidst the gusty winds that blow through this pass.

The hostel El Portal is situated on the crest of a peak, serving *bocadillos* and coffee to the pilgrims. The Pilgrim sipped a *cafe con leche* and stood on the edge of the summit, overlooking the world. It was a magically golden world full of brilliant blue and puffy white. Watching in stunned silence, the magnificent beauty of the morning sunlight rose above the sea of heavy rolling clouds shrouding everything but the distant mountain island peaks in mystery. The Pilgrim dreamt momentarily of embarking on a weightless journey in the lightest of ships to sail into the horizon on the wispy veneer of these flowing billows. But one cannot allow their head to stay in the clouds. Indeed, we must submit to the gravity of the situation and keep our feet on the ground below, for this path was made for walking, not floating. And walk on we must.

Westward, the path begins to drop in altitude. While there will inevitably be more slopes along the way, we are now leaving the mountains. The landscape itself begins to whisper the unavoidable truth, that the journey to Santiago de Compostela is nearing an end. But not to fear, there is plenty of time to stop and smell the roses and taste the local *freixós*, a traditional cake-type pastry made like flan, except flour and anise are added to the mix. Overhead fly harrier, sparrow hawk, raven, and *choughs* (pronounced "CHUF"), a rare blackbird with a red beak that pairs with its mate for life.

The rapid taps of the Great Spotted Woodpecker can be heard and flashes of the tiny yellow Firecrest warbler can be seen in the bushes near the stonewalled *San Pedro*, the smallest church building along the Camino. Each pilgrim will pass an ancient chestnut tree in the village of Ramil whose branches have been growing for more than 800 years!

Finally, the pilgrims reach Triacastela built along the Oribio River which is contoured by a riparian forest of familiar trees of chestnut, poplars, and oak. The town receives its name from three tenth-century castles that previously existed here, but are no longer standing. Their rubble was probably used to construct local houses or the local Galician style hedges made with vertical slabs of stone.

Camino Contemplation

As Saint James concludes his writing over the next few days, he reiterates and summarizes the message he intends to instill in us, his fellow disciples in Christ. He emphasizes the importance of patience as a virtue, and reminds us that complaining against each other gets us nowhere in life.

The demigods of this age temp us to bring curses to the peoples of the world through hurtful words and negative thoughts. We would do well to avoid these temptations and even go actively resist them. By God's grace, these devils flee when we resist because of the blood of Christ.

Our journey on the Camino is entering its final days, yet there is still much to learn along the way. As we tread wearily upon the earth, let us remember to walk in patience, without complaining, trusting that Christ is working within us to make us more virtuous through His sacrifice on the Cross.

Practical Application

Patience is a virtue. So is blessing your friends and family.

St. James Writes

James 5 : 7 *So be patient, brothers, until the Lord's coming. See, the farmer awaits the valuable harvest from the ground. He is patiently waiting for it, until it receives the early and late rains.* **8** *You, too, be patient. Make your hearts strong, because the Lord's coming is near.* **9** *Do not complain, brothers, against one another, so that you will be not judged. See, the judge is standing at the door.*

Prayer for the Peregrino

Dear Lord, thank you for instilling Your life in me. Help me not to complain, nor be bitter. I humbly ask that Your grace be with me as I learn patience from You. Thank you for being trustworthy.

In Christ's Name, Amen.

TWENTY-SIXTH DAY

"Carry as little as possible, but choose that little with care."

- Earl Schaffer, first thru-hiker of the
Appalachian Trail in the USA

The Path from Triacastela to Sarria

The road from Triacastela to Sarria offers two options for pilgrims. The traditional route is more direct, but most pilgrims seem to prefer the longer alternative route that takes them through a small and ancient town called Samos. It is here that one of the largest and oldest of the Benedictine monasteries in Spain lies at the bottom of a quiet and dreamy valley on the banks of the Sarria River.

Housed within the Baroque facade of this quiet sixth-century abbey is a large basilica with two monasteries. This place is known for having hosted both royalty and peasants, saints and sinners throughout the ages. It was once utilized as a war hospital in the ninth century. Its design is complete with a refectory for communal meals, an impressive library, and even a cloister garden within the monastery walls serving as a *garth*, or inner sanctum. It is the perfect space for contemplation, prayer, and perhaps a pinch of herb or sample of fruit.

It is here in the monastery with its massive library of books that one can find a statue of the Spanish monk who was a scholarly thought leader of his day. This monk helped lead the Enlightenment in Spain. Father Feijóo wrote about the beauty of the Samos Valley when he said, "The disposition of the place portrays the religion of its inhabitants, portrays it and still influences it, because the horizon is closed on all sides, there are no objects where the spirit can dissipate. You can only look heavenward."

Perhaps one might feel claustrophobic if only staying in the valley. But for the pilgrim who is only passing through Samos, the nestled area is perceived to be a cozy and fertile paradise.

Crossing the Almirón bridge, happy pilgrims, although somewhat reluctant to move on from this idyllic little town, take their leave of Samos and begin the steep climb out of the valley, which is surrounded by the El Carballal and La Modorra Mountains. And our gaze is indeed drawn heavenward.

From there, pilgrims follow the gorge through verdant forests of unfolding ferns and moss-covered oaks. Darting to and fro, wild quail and partridge might be seen plucking bugs from the tufts of bushes. The path continues towards the Pedrafita Mountains, past tiny hamlets with Galician names like Foxos, Teiguín, and Frollais.

If you look closely, you might be able to spot the iconic red-capped toadstool mushroom growing in the forest floors, spotted with white on the dome. In the grasslands outside the forests, pilgrims will walk past curious grazing cows kept in by columns of stone fences.

Once upon a time, pilgrims would gather a limestone rock or two from the area and carry it with them to Santiago to help with the building of the Cathedral of Santiago. In this way, thousands of pilgrims of old have been able to play a small part in building the icon of the Camino.

The sound of the Camino has changed over the centuries. Today, as pilgrims pass each other, we say "Buen Camino" as both a blessing and greeting to our fellow pilgrims, wishing them a good journey or pilgrimage.

However, this has not always been the case. Almost a thousand years ago, as revealed in the twelfth-century Codex Calixtinus, pilgrims would greet each other with the phrase "¡Ultreïa!" meaning "Onward!" in its simplest form. Pilgrims would respond with "¡E suseïa!" meaning "And upward!" An additional Latin saying would then be exchanged by both parties: "Deus adjuva nos!" meaning "May God help us!" Ultimately, it was a way to encourage one another to keep on going!

While the original language of these two old proto-Romanic words, "ultreïa" and "suseïa", remains obscure, remnants can still be found along the way. It is possible that it was a pidgin expression formed as a result of people from various linguistic backgrounds attempting to communicate with one another. In a pidgin vocabulary, people find a common way to say something that blends the languages together without actually creating an entirely new and complete language. Some new mother tongues, called creole languages, are complete languages that have developed having once started as a simple pidgin.

The local Galician language (sometimes disapprovingly referred to as *Castrapo*) is one such creole, as it is a mix of mainly Latin and Portuguese with the incorporation of Celtic, Germanic, and Spanish loanwords.

Today, these melodic words from the Codex Calixtinus can still be heard sung in the "Song of the Pilgrims of Santiago": "Ultreia, ultreia! E suseia! Deus adjuva nos!"

Camino Contemplation

One of the lessons we learn on the Camino is endurance. We suffer along the way with soreness, pain, hunger, and other challenges that arise.

Saint James reminds us that those who endure hardships and trials are considered blessed. He knows they are blessed because they learn to rejoice in their sufferings, knowing that suffering produces endurance. Endurance produces character, and character produces hope (anticipation with pleasure). Hope does not disappoint because the love of God is poured into our hearts through the Holy Spirit who was given to us as a gift (see Romans 5). C. S. Lewis defined hope as "a continual looking forward to the eternal world".

As we journey along the Camino, let us remember that God is teaching us endurance, which makes us blessed because we trust in Him. He is good and loves us with an unfailing love. May God help us endure to the end!

Practical Application

We must endure the pain of the path in order to reach the end. But in this we are blessed with endurance and other fruits of the Holy Spirit.

St. James Writes

James 5 : 10 *Take an example, brothers, from the suffering and patience of the prophets, those who spoke in the name of the Lord.* ***11*** *See, we regard those who endured as blessed. You have heard of the endurance of Job, and you know the purpose of the Lord, how he is very compassionate and merciful.*

Prayer for the Peregrino

Dear Lord, thank you for Your compassion and mercy toward me and my fellow pilgrims. May Your grace sustain me as I learn to endure the hardships. I trust You that you are working something good in me.

In Christ's Name, Amen.

TWENTY-SEVENTH DAY

"Walking is the exact balance between spirit and humility."

- Gary Snyder, American poet

The Path from Sarria to Portomarín

At every hostel and place of interest along the way, pilgrims unfailingly present their elongated credencial de peregrino, or pilgrim's passport, to receive a notary stamp of certification. Their passports are now filled with imprints of every place they have visited along the way. To be eligible for the certificate of completion at the end of the journey, a minimum distance of 100 kilometers from Santiago de Compostela must have been covered.

Some pilgrims opt for a shorter journey and seek to complete it within a week. For those on foot, horseback, or bicycle who have chosen the French Way, Sarria in Lugo province is often the starting point. At the wall beneath the Iglesia de Santa María in Sarria, the foot traffic noticeably increases.

Leaving Sarria, pilgrims pass by an old prison and gradually pass through a beautiful oak grove along the Camino. It is a simple and sometimes muddy walk up and down rural green slopes and fields. The route takes us through ancient enclaves, rustic outcroppings of meadows, and rows of brambles of rose, blackberry, and occasionally gorse. Gorse, a yellow-flowering plant with green stems and small leaves, has an excessive amount of thorns. Stone houses, stone hedges, and simple stone churches dot the landscape. Some of these churches have nests that can be seen in corners of the bell towers, possibly belonging to barn owls.

The most notable church here is the 12th-century Church of Saint James, the Igrexa de Santiago de Barbadelo, which is a national monument of unique importance due to its Galician Romanesque architecture. While passing through Galicia, the structures of the small village churches are simple stone buildings built for durability, lacking adornment or decoration. But in Barbadelo, an attempt has been made to enhance the exterior of the building. Aficionados of architecture will appreciate the tympanum, the front, and the north side, with interesting figures of mysterious animals, scallop shells, roses, a figure of flagellated Christ, a Celtic-style laced knot, pinecones, and other complex human representations crafted into the stone.

The Camino continues under the shade of oak, chestnut, and birch trees. These clusters interweave through rural farms and spread out over the countryside hills in verdant swirls of shaded celebration for each pilgrim. The landscape gradually transitions into hardened granite from the hills of grainy schist and smooth slate. The fields reflect the lessening of agriculture while towns become larger and closer together. Crosses of wood, stone, and metal stand erect along the way as constant reminders that we are indeed pilgrims on a journey that leads to life in Christ.

The sense of the journey gradually morphs. It's a change that will gradually draw the pilgrim into the future. While passing under the shade of Middle Earth-style tree tunnels, Saint Augustine's words echo in our minds, "Who can deny that things to come are not yet? Yet already there is in the mind an expectation of things to come." We are challenged to remain present, and each step forward is a step in the right direction. While the mind may look forward to the end of the journey, we must embrace the mystery and awe of the present moment.

While we certainly do not wish for the journey to conclude, there is a healthy tension in this crisis that burns up any negative thoughts, resulting in a special clarity of who we are and how we are to live.

Somewhere outside the town of Sarria lies the hamlet of Brea, where a marker stands, signifying that there are only 100 kilometers left in the pilgrim's journey. Due to its proximity to the marker, Sarria is the natural starting point for both hikers and cyclists, who have an additional 20 kilometers to complete to receive their certificate of completion from the Office of the Peregrino in Santiago de Compostela, still a couple of days away.

Moving along through the verdant forests, the soft rustle of the leaves and the gentle murmur of the flowing creeks create a serene and peaceful atmosphere. The meadows stretch out as far as the eye can see. They are painted with a palette of vibrant greens, dotted with colorful wildflowers and grazing animals. It's as if nature is alive and speaking to us, declaring the glory of God, and beckoning us to pause and take it all in. We are humbled by the natural beauty that surrounds us and can't help but feel a sense of wonder and awe.

It is a truly wonderful part of the journey as we look forward to the celebration at the end, but first, we must pass through Portomarín.

Camino Contemplation

Saint James was one of the closest disciples of Jesus, and he learned how to live by walking with Him. As modern-day pilgrims, we too can follow in James' footsteps and walk with Christ. The teachings of Saint James offer practical ways to emulate the life of Jesus and to live a life of integrity.

Jesus showed us how to walk the straight and narrow path, and it is through our daily conversations and interactions that we have the chance to show our own integrity. Saint James reminds us to be true to our word and to avoid making empty promises. We must mean what we say and say what we mean. By doing so, we show others that we are trustworthy and reliable.

As we journey along the Camino, let us reflect on our own words and actions, and ask Christ for the strength to live with integrity. It is through our commitment to truth and honesty that we can deepen our relationship with God and with our fellow pilgrims. Let us remember the example set by Saint James and strive to walk as Christ walked, with love and compassion for all those we meet along the way.

Practical Application

Be a person of your word.

St. James Writes

James 5 : 12 *But above all, my brothers, do not swear, either by heaven or by the earth, or by any other oath. Instead, let your "Yes" mean "Yes" and your "No" mean "No," so you do not fall under judgment.*

Prayer for the Peregrino

Dear Lord, thank you for keeping Your promises. I humbly ask that You help me to walk with the same integrity that You walked in. Thank you for giving me Your strength and showing me the way of righteousness.

In Christ's Name, Amen.

TWENTY-EIGHTH DAY

"To move, to breath, to fly, to float, To gain all while you give, To roam the roads of lands remote, To travel is to live."

- Hans Christian Anderson, Danish author

Portomarín

The yellow arrows have been constant companions to the pilgrims on their journey. They have been found painted, sketched, and colored onto anything that will last, including tree trunks, fence posts, and the abundant granite stone that makes up most of the walls of Portomarín and other towns in the region.

These arrows are an integral part of the Pilgrim's journey, guiding them towards their destination. But, the yellow arrows were not always present on the Camino. It was not until the late 1900s that a priest from O Cebreiro, Elías Valiña, introduced the yellow arrows. His in-depth study of the Camino's history led him to retrace the journey from the beginning of the French Route, painting yellow arrows along the way. While the reason behind the choice of yellow as the color and where he obtained the paint is not certain, the color has proven to be a suitable hue, easily visible across the countryside. Prior to the implementation of the yellow arrows, the path was challenging to navigate.

Various crosses placed in seemingly haphazard locations along the way, along with stone monoliths, and later, arrow-shaped rock piles were the primary symbols leading the way. For centuries, people could easily become lost and perish in the wilderness, especially during extreme seasonal conditions.

Today, the arrow has become an iconic symbol of the Camino. Its widespread use makes it almost impossible to lose one's way, at least for long. We owe a debt of gratitude to Elías, who devoted his life to reviving the path of the pilgrim, making it feasible for millions of pilgrims to travel to Santiago de Compostela.

As pilgrims approach Portomarín, they must first cross the long and high bridge over the southern flowing Miño River, an essential source of trout and eels, before entering the town. At times, when the water level is high, pilgrims can be seen jumping into the cold and refreshing waters below, near the "Do Not Jump from Bridge" signage.

In the late 1950s, the dam at Embalse de Belesar, some 20 plus miles downstream, would be built and cause Portomarín's old town to flood and ultimately be submerged by the dam waters. But before this happened and during the dam's construction, the buildings of utmost importance were numbered stone by stone, disassembled, relocated, and finally rebuilt nearby.

During the dry seasons, the original Roman bridge and remains of buildings, as well as a small landing pier, can be seen protruding through the mud. The area was originally inhabited by the peoples of the Castro culture (*cultura castrexa*), whose almost 2,200-year-old hill-forts and other settlement ruins can be found in abundance in the region.

As we approach Portomarín, two yellow arrows point in opposite directions just before entering the town. We are faced with a choice: to climb a series of daunting stairs leading from the bridge or to take the alternate path to the right, which adds extra steps. Most pilgrims choose to walk the longer path to get into town.

Once we enter the town square, we are greeted by the magnificent Church of Saint Nicholas, which boasts a large cuboid frame and massive round rose window situated between two corner towers. The building is a fortified castle-church, constructed as both a sanctuary for the soul and a fortress utilized by the military, and its Romanesque style is flanked by a semicircular apse.

The Church of Saint Nicholas is a testament to the resilience of the people of Portomarín, who were able to rebuild their town in the face of certain destruction. The visible numbers carved into the building stones for relocation serve as a reminder of the town's history and the Pilgrim's journey.

Camino Contemplation

As followers of Christ, we know that we are not perfect and that we need a Healer to help us along our spiritual journey. It's important to recognize that sometimes we need physical healing, while at other times we need healing for the internal things such as our minds, wills, and emotions. Saint James teaches us the importance of prayer, joyful singing, asking for prayer, confessing our sins to one another, and praying for each other. Although confessing our sins to others can be difficult and humiliating, it can also bring life to our hearts and lead to healing.

As we walk our path, let us be open to receiving and offering prayer for healing for ourselves and others. Let us find the courage to ask someone to pray for us and to offer mercy to those we meet who may be in need of healing. When we pray in faith, we can trust that God will fulfill His promise and bring about healing.

It's important to remember that our response to the things that happen and the depth of our spiritual community directly affects the health of our spiritual life. Let us strive to build a strong community of faith and to respond to life's challenges with grace and trust in God's plan for us.

Practical Application

Our response to things that happen and the depth of our

spiritual community directly affects the health of our spiritual life.

St. James Writes

James 5 : 13 *Is anyone among you suffering hardship? Let him pray. Is anyone cheerful? Let him sing praise.* **14** *Is anyone among you sick? Let him call for the elders of the church, and let them pray over him. Let them anoint him with oil in the name of the Lord.* **15** *The prayer of faith will heal the sick person, and the Lord will raise him up. If he has committed sins, God will forgive him.* **16** *So confess your sins to one another, and pray for each other, so that you may be healed.*

Prayer for the Peregrino

Dear Lord, thank you for setting an example for me. You prayed for strength and You weren't afraid to pray for others and with others. Help me to walk in faith and pray bold prayers. Help me to sing joyful songs and not songs of darkness. Help me to walk humbly and confess to my mature brothers and sisters that I may find healing in You, the Great Healer.

In Christ's Name, Amen.

TWENTY-NINETH DAY

"Strong and content I travel the open road."

- Walt Whitman, Nineteenth-century US poet

The Path from Portomarín to Palace de Rei

As the Pilgrim trudged along the Camino de Santiago, he wondered how much longer he could endure. The wilderness seemed never-ending, and the next town felt impossibly far away. Just then, he spotted a lone wooden cart ahead of him. Although it was the middle of nowhere, someone was giving away snacks and drinks to weary pilgrims passing by.

Approaching the cart, the Pilgrim felt a sense of bewilderment. Who was this man and why was he giving away all the food? The man just smiled and offered him hot tea and an apple. There were bananas and cookies and biscuits, and a lot more! The invitation to rest was gratefully accepted.

Was this man an angel in disguise, sent to provide the pilgrims with the strength needed to continue on their journey? Or was he just a kind-hearted stranger, embodying the spirit of Christ and the Camino itself? Is there a difference? Whoever he was, he brought great encouragement to everyone who passed by. The pilgrim ate the last of his biscuit, sipped the last of his hot tea, and thanked the man before continuing down the road. This was an unexpected moment of grace. Further down the road, he paused to glance back at the lone man with the wooden cart that was disappearing behind him. He may never know the full story of this stranger, but the memory of his generosity would stay with him for the rest of his life.

Outside of Portomarín, the Pilgrim passed through the quaint village of Toxibo. A waist-high wall runs along the path, and just beyond it lies an oddly shaped building, tall and slender. It is another hórreo, the traditional Galician granary with a thin wooden frame, raised off the ground by a large stone footing and *staddle* stone pillars.

As the Pilgrim ventures deeper into the Iberian Peninsula, the terrain takes on a reddish hue, and the dirt paths underfoot are studded with chunks of metamorphic *gneiss*. The landscape is rolling, not as ruggedly mountainous like before. It continues with lush trees, plentiful hostels, and local eateries. Signs of modern technology and design are everywhere, marking the increasing pulse of human activity.

However, as the end of the journey draws near, the pilgrims sense a shift in the air. Thoughts of post-pilgrimage life creep in, tempting them to revert to old patterns. But now, more than ever, it is essential to stay focused and mindful, keeping Christ's teachings close to heart and cherishing the new friends made along the way. The journey is not yet over.

The hillsides are rich with moss and bracken, interspersed with cornfields, oak trees, and eucalyptus forests. The eucalyptus trees are not native so they are used in lumber and paper products. Thickets of broom, gorse, and heather bloom along the way, providing shelter for the colorful red, black, and white Stonechats as well as Dartford warblers with their red eyes and long thin tails. Additionally, Dunnock, with their greenish-grayish heads, and migratory Whitethroats with their reddish stains on their wings, flit about, collecting berries, flies, and grubs for their young. Thickets of bamboo appear randomly, adding to the picturesque scenery.

Camino Contemplation

Saint James living as one of Christ's original disciples understood that the sacrificial work of Jesus on the cross brings us into a state of approval with God. We become righteous and innocent because of Jesus Christ, the Way of salvation. Jesus emphasized the importance of faith, saying that even if our faith is as small as a mustard seed (which is smaller than a watermelon seed), we can move mountains. Saint James highlights the faith of a patriarch, showing us that we too can have this kind of faith, even if we don't hold the title of "saint".

As we near the end of our journey, we must continue to walk in faith, trusting in the integrity and character of God. We must pray with boldness for the things we need, like more of His presence within us. God hears our prayers and works through us to bring goodness and peace to our lives and those around us.

Faith is not always easy, but it is a deep conviction of trusting in God. Saint James knew this from walking with Christ and understood that sometimes our prayers are not answered because there is something broken and hidden within us. Confession is the act of revealing our brokenness, and it can be humiliating. However, God gives grace to the humble, and when we shine His light on our darkness, God's grace sweeps in to bring healing and restoration.

Jesus Christ is the Great Physician and desires to heal both our physical bodies and inner beings. Confession to a mature disciple and prayer in faith can lead to holistic healing of our spirit, soul, mind, and body.

As we walk with Christ, let us walk in humility and grace, praying with each other in faith so that we may be healed. May we trust in God's character and integrity, knowing that He is faithful to keep His Word.

Practical Application

Prayer and confession are essential for healing.

St. James Writes

James 5 : 15 *The prayer of faith will heal the sick person, and the Lord will raise him up. If he has committed sins, God will forgive him.* **16** *So confess your sins to one another, and pray for each other, so that you may be healed.*

Prayer for the Peregrino

Dear Lord, thank you for healing my mind, body, soul, and spirit. Help me to pray in faith, without doubting because You are trustworthy and reliable.

In Christ's Name, Amen.

THIRTIETH DAY

"The world reveals itself to those who travel on foot."

- Werner Herzog, German film director

The Path from Palace de Rei, to Arzúa (Ribadiso)

The Pilgrim has reached the last full day of walking along the Camino de Santiago. It is a day that each pilgrim who has traveled from the beginning has been looking forward to. This journey has taken the pilgrims through the verdant countryside of Galicia teeming with blooming wildflowers, fields of heather, sporadic ferns, and blackberry bushes. The pilgrimage has taken each pilgrim through quiet forests growing with narrow-leafed ash, fragrant pines, whisky willows, and temperate birch. They have trekked through dairy country, tasted local soft cheese, white Albariño wines, and perhaps have sampled the local Gallego fare called *Octopus á Feira*.

There have been many bird sightings, and they may have caught a glimpse of a fox or deer along the way. The earth has yielded crops in vegetable gardens and deposits of clay utilized by kilns and straw stored in haylofts. Old farm tools and *brona*, ovens for cornbread, have been dispersed throughout tiny villages, hamlets, and ancient settlements.

The town of Castañeda just before Arzúa is where pilgrims of old deposited their limestone rocks from Triacastela. Here it was put into the giant kilns where it was then turned into lime used for the construction of the Cathedral in Santiago.

They have glimpsed more of the raised hórreo granaries. Some have been open, and the corn can be seen drying inside. The smaller-sized ones made of wood and thatch are called a cabazo. The Pilgrims have walked over ancient bridges that stretch over countless small rivers and streams. They've walked past orchards of sweet and fleshy fruit. Each eye has gazed upon the innumerable Romanesque structures, coats of arms, ornate baroque façades, and stone churches, each giving glory to the Creator in its own expressive way, whether simple or extravagant. Indeed, we are realizing in humility that each act of worship is extravagant in the eyes of God.

In Arzúa, the last major town before Santiago, the Camino del Norte converges with the French Way. The Monte de Gozo, or Mount Joy, is the last hill in Pedrouzo before the absolute final descent into Santiago de Compostela. From this height, the pilgrim can get a panoramic glimpse of the magnificent city of Santiago de Compostela.

Camino Contemplation

One of the scariest things about embarking on a journey is the possibility of getting lost. Sometimes, the fear is felt by the person who is lost, but other times it's the person who loves them who is more afraid. Saint James recognized that in our journey on Earth, we can lose our way. But the good news is that Christ comes to find us. When we are found by Christ, we can declare that we have found the path of Salvation because of the truth of Christ. There are many paths that lead to Christ, but only one path leads to "Our Father who art in Heaven." Jesus Christ is that path. He even reveals to us that He Himself is the Way, the Truth, and the Life. Christ teaches us that no one can come to God the Father except through Him. (See John 14:6)

Christ called Himself the Good Shepherd. Lost sheep, no matter how they became lost, are more vulnerable to wolves who would try to kill and eat them, or to anyone who would steal that sheep for their own selfish gain. Christ said that He came to seek and save those who are lost. Through the Holy Spirit of Christ, His disciples become His hands and feet, helping to bring the lost ones back to Him. It is a community effort in which God works with humankind to bring redemption.

As we near the end of our journey on the Camino de Santiago, let us ensure that we are found in Christ. Once we have found Him, let us join Him in His mission and help Him seek and save other lost sheep. This is how we become most like Christ. To walk the way of Saint James is to walk the Way of Christ Himself.

Practical Application

We are righteous because of Christ, therefore our prayers are powerful.

St. James Writes

James 5 : 16 *The prayer of a righteous person is very strong in its working.* **17** *Elijah was a man just like us. He prayed earnestly that it would not rain, and it did not rain in the land for three years and six months.* **18** *Then Elijah prayed again, and the heavens gave rain, and the earth produced its fruit.*

Prayer for the Peregrino

Dear Lord, thank you for making me righteous in Christ. I pray that You help me to walk in faith and to pray with boldness for the things I need to help me build goodness in Your Kingdom. Thank you for being there for me.

In Christ's Name, Amen.

THIRTY-FIRST DAY

> "You never know what's around the corner. It could be everything. Or it could be nothing. You keep putting one food in front of the other, and then one day you look back and you've climbed a mountain."
>
> - Tom Hiddleston, English actor

Santiago de Compostela

There is no fanfare or paparazzi for anyone as they enter the destination city of their pilgrimage. The city is as beautiful as any of the towns of recent days.

Suddenly, there it is, the Cathedral of Santiago. It stands stalwart, resolute, reaching towards the heavens, bearing a sense of dignity. It stands in beautiful solemnity to welcome each weary traveler. It feels like…home. Albeit a home where we have never been before. Congratulations are in order as new found friends clasp each other with wide grins and tears of joy. They've made it, together.

And together the pilgrims in Obradoiro Plaza ascend the steps, each placing their hand onto the marble column just before the entrance. Over many centuries, countless numbers of pilgrims have also placed their hands in this same spot leaving a permanent imprint of a hand. Quietly, each pilgrim enters into the darkened cathedral, kneeling to say a prayer of gratitude, possibly embracing the statute of the saint, and finally descending into the holy sepulcher where a silver chest sits protected behind bars. Within this trunk rests the relics of our beloved Saint James, Apostle of Jesus Christ.

And just like that, our quest is complete.

Camino Contemplation

The Camino is a pilgrimage, a type of intentional wandering. It is a reflection of our spiritual journey lived out in the physical journey we experience during our time on earth.

Saint James knew this and concludes his writings with a final thought about wandering. The focus is on those who wander away from faith, from the truth of Christ. He admonishes us all to humble ourselves and attempt to guide back to faith the one who has wandered away.

Ultimately, it is Christ who is the guide, but he uses each of us as the cup to pour the healing waters of truth to revive the weary soul. Indeed, the very writings of Saint James are reflective of this as he writes with great urgency.

It is both a warning and an encouragement. First, do not wander aimlessly without the guidance of Christ. Second, you can help find the lost sheep and bring them back into the Shepherd's fold.

And just as we have made it to the end of our journey along the Way of Saint James, so we find ourselves now grateful for the many others who have guided us during our wanderings of recent days. It is now we find ourselves at our intended destination. It is now that we find ourselves home.

Practical Application

Our role is to help bring the wandering ones back.

St. James Writes

James 5 : 19 *My brothers, if anyone among you wanders from the truth, and someone brings him back,* **20** *that person should know* *that whoever turns a sinner from his wandering way will save his soul from death, and will cover over a great number of sins.*

Prayer for the Peregrino

Dear Lord, thank you for finding me. Help me, I pray, to not wander away from You. I also ask that You would use me as an instrument of mercy to help bring another lost sheep back into safety and salvation in You. Thank you for being my Good Shepherd.

In Christ's Name, Amen.

CONCLUSION

"We are all compelled by a yearning for eternity - by the possibility of the divine."

- Seth Barnes, Founder of Adventures.org

Cape Finisterre, the End of the World

Where will you go now?

Some pilgrims continue to walk after receiving their Compostela in Santiago. Those pilgrims who walk to the end of the world will find themselves in Cape Finisterre overlooking the mighty waters of the Atlantic Ocean. While it is not required, the walk can be completed in about three additional days.

For some, there is a sense of loss at the end of the journey. But the loss is bittersweet. While we leave the mud and dust from the Camino behind us, we also celebrate the milestone of moving on renewed in our life. And I think that maybe that is a good perspective on death.

While there is a time of mourning, the celebration of the accomplishment of a journey completed to the best of our abilities takes the sting out of the bitterness. But for pilgrims, we know that the path is only beginning. And we have learned how life is itself a spiritual journey. Therefore, we move forward stronger, our path taking us on the upward path towards our final home of peace.

Jesus Christ initially called twelve disciples to Himself. Those twelve people expanded into dozens of men and women, and then hundreds, and eventually into millions of people who, throughout the ages, have felt that call within themselves. These are the ones who have left everything that tied them down and became disciples of Christ. Those original twelve disciples eventually became sent by Christ and were called *apostles*, which means "sent ones," having a similar position as modern political ambassadors.

In the early years after the death, burial, and resurrection of Christ Jesus, other disciples learned the calling of Jesus. It is this mandate that commands them to go into all the world and teach others to be disciples of Jesus Christ, to baptize them in the name of the Father, the Son, and the Holy Spirit, and to teach them to obey all that Jesus commanded. (See Matthew 28) They became apostles or sent ones; ambassadors of the Kingdom of God.

From the teachings of Saint James and the other disciples, apostles, and saints, we learn that it is not enough to simply be a follower of Christ. We must choose to learn from Christ and then obey what He teaches.

At the end of the day, it is all about love: loving ourselves well, loving others well, and loving God well. Without love, liturgy becomes lifeless. Without love, religion becomes an addictive opiate. Without love, our lives dry up and become like an empty desert wasteland.

We are to fear God, and because perfect love casts out fear, we are free to love Him. And because God loves us and bought us back from Death by the death of His only begotten Son, Jesus, we are adopted as sons and daughters into God's family. This means that Jesus is like our brother, as it says in Romans 8:29!

As a son or daughter of the King of Kings, you can rest in confidence knowing that God loves you, and nothing can separate you from His love. Don't focus on all the dark things around the world. Focus on Christ alone, and how you are seen as righteous as Christ in the eyes of God! Anyone can focus on how we were born as sinners; in fact, that's all that religion is good at. But while we were still sinners, Christ died for us, purchasing us with His blood, and now our bloodline is the same as God's, making us co-heirs with Christ! And that is the Gospel.

As our journey in life continues, like Saint James of old, let us walk with Christ in purity of heart, in humility of action, and in constant meditation of whatever is honorable, whatever is just, whatever is pure, whatever is lovely, whatever is of good report, and if anything is excellent, and if anything is praiseworthy. (See Philippians 4:8)

We have finished the writings of Saint James and will conclude with what Saint Paul wrote.

St. Paul Writes

1 Corinthians 13:13 But now these three remain: faith, hope, and love. But the greatest of these is love.

Final Prayer for the Peregrino

Dear Lord, thank you for giving me the strength to walk this Camino de Santiago. Thank you for the friends I've met along the way. Thank you for helping me to persevere and to walk in humility. As my journey here comes to an end, I pray Lord, that You would continue to guide me. And may I live in the light and truth of Your love.

In Christ's Name, Amen.

AFTERWORD

"With God there are no wasted journeys."

- Elliot Clark

A pilgrimage is a sacred journey of intentional wandering, a paradox where getting lost helps us find ourselves in Christ.

The Camino de Santiago is said to have three main stages: physical, mental, and spiritual.

In his seminal work "Kingdom Journeys, Rediscovering the Lost Spiritual Discipline", Seth Barnes notes that every journey also has three main stages of development. The first stage is *abandonment*, where we learn to abandon our past, ourselves, and anything we would hold onto for comfort. The second stage is *brokenness*, where we feel the loss of that which we abandoned. This stage is challenging to get through, but God will guide us to the other side. It is in this stage that we begin to learn what it means to be human, see the world in a new light, and embrace humility.

The third stage is dependence, where we learn to depend upon God alone for everything that we need, and to embrace only things that truly matter in life.

The Camino de Santiago has been a holy pilgrimage for over a millennium, and millions of pilgrims have journeyed through its various networks of paths, going through the sacred process of abandonment, brokenness, and dependence along the way.

Our journey together through the writings of Saint James has been immersive. We have all felt the calling to embark on the Camino, prompted by a sense of dissatisfaction with the existing state of affairs in our lives, and longing to find fulfillment. The Camino has proven that our searching is not meaningless; quite the opposite, really.

Seth Barnes calls this longing for something more the "gift of restlessness." Through restlessness, God pushes us into abandoning our normal lives and getting physically broken with many hours and miles hiked along the Camino. As we choose to take each step forward, we learn dependency on God and our fellow pilgrims. This is the way of journeying with Christ, and a process that God will use in our lives to refine and purify our hearts.

The Camino de Santiago is also a sacred quest, personal to each of us. But Santiago de Compostela is not the ultimate destination; it's a step along the journey of life. Only by walking alongside Christ, as Saint James did, will we ever find our quest fulfilled. And only in Christ will we ever reach our destination satisfied and whole.

Dear pilgrim, your journey is only beginning. May God's shalom-peace be upon you as you continue walking alongside Christ, refining and purifying your heart. Amen.

Zebulun Mattos, Spring 2023

The author wishes to thank the following authors and bloggers whose works have greatly enhanced both the understanding of the Camino de Santiago and what it means to be a pilgrim.

- Gitlitz, David and Linda Kay Davidson. *The Pilgrimage Road to Santiago: The Complete Cultural Handbook.* New York: St. Martin's Press, 2000

- Barnes, Seth. *Kingdom Journeys: Rediscovering the Lost Spiritual Discipline.* USA: Ashland Press, 2012 sethbarnes.com

- Everard, Jerry. www.thefogwatch.com/camino-de-santiago-french-route/ (accessed April, 2023)

- Gilmour, Leslie. www.caminoadventures.com/camino-maps/ (accessed April, 2023)

- www.galiciaguide.com/Camino-de-Santiago.html (accessed April, 2023)

My heart is full of gratitude for the following people:

Candace, my love, thank you for encouraging me throughout the process. You're my favorite!

Bernice Mattos, my mother, Thank you for helping with the editing and for raising me to follow Jesus.

Lonnie Mattos, my dad, thank you for encouraging me to always seek bigger fish.

Ephraim Mattos, my own brother, thank you for your insights which helped guide me through the publication process.

Megan and Kyle Kappe, thank you for proofreading the early versions of the text. And thank you for being good examples of what it looks like to bridge liturgical faith with modern life.

Seth Barnes, thank you for taking a chance and believing in me. Your initial feedback was critical to the development of this work.

Kingdom Journeys friends and mentors on the *Camino de Santiago*: Seth, Mac, Justin, Hugh, Sunoh, Daniel, Colby, Neil, Dusty, David, Damon, Glenn, and Fabio.

Also, a special thanks to the people and government of Spain, and the Office of the Pilgrim (oficinadelperegrino.com) for doing such an amazing job at hosting the *Camino de Santiago* for millions of pilgrims around the world. We couldn't do it without you.

Zebulun Mattos, NREMT, is an avid adventurer, travel writer, and chef. Since 2010, he has traveled to over 30 countries living and working alongside local humanitarian organizations and communities of faith.

He lives in the USA with his wife, Candace, an ASL teacher. Together they founded *Harbor's Light International*, a philanthropic nonprofit established to revive the human spirit by restoring *faith* in humanity, cultivating *hope* for a better future, and demonstrating *love* by caring for people in need around the world.

HarborsLight.org

For more publications by the author, you
can visit www.ZebulunMattos.com

May the road rise up to meet you.
May the wind be always at your back.
May the sun shine warm upon your face,
and rains fall soft upon your cheeks.
And until we meet again, may God hold you in the palm of his hand.
We ask this through Jesus Christ our Lord. Amen.

- Traditional Irish Prayer